FEDERAL RULES OF EVIDENCE 2025 EDITION

With Advisory Committee Notes, Internal Cross-References, Statutory and Landmark Case Supplement | Recent Amendments and Practical Exercises

ProCore Mastery

DISCLAIMER

This study guide provides general information about the Federal Rules of Evidence. While every effort has been made to ensure accuracy, the law evolves constantly. This material should supplement, not replace, thorough legal research and professional judgment in actual practice.

TABLE OF CONTENTS

PREFACE

HOW TO USE THIS STUDY GUIDE

This study guide provides a systematic approach to mastering the Federal Rules of Evidence for law school examinations, bar preparation, and courtroom practice. The Federal Rules of Evidence govern the admissibility of evidence in federal courts and serve as the foundation for evidence law in most state jurisdictions.

Organization and Structure

Each chapter follows a consistent analytical framework designed to facilitate both comprehension and practical application:

1. Rule Analysis: Each rule is presented with its complete text, followed by essential elements and requirements.
2. Doctrinal Framework: Key concepts are organized hierarchically, progressing from foundational principles to specific applications.
3. Practical Applications: Real-world examples and hypothetical scenarios demonstrate how courts apply these rules in practice.

- Strategic Considerations: Practice tips address common pitfalls and tactical considerations for effective advocacy.

Recommended Study Approach

1. Phase One - Foundation Building: Begin with Chapter 1 to establish conceptual understanding of relevance, reliability, and the analytical framework underlying all evidence rules.
2. Phase Two - Rule Mastery: Study each subsequent chapter systematically, focusing on the interplay between related rules rather than memorizing isolated provisions.
3. Phase Three - Application Practice: Utilize the practice problems and review materials to develop analytical proficiency and issue-spotting skills.

Examination Strategy

For law school examinations, focus on the analytical process rather than rote memorization. Evidence professors typically test your ability to:

- Identify evidence issues quickly and accurately
- Apply the appropriate legal standard
- Analyze competing policy considerations
- Reach reasoned conclusions under time pressure

For bar examination preparation, emphasize the most frequently tested rules identified in the Quick Reference section below, while maintaining sufficient breadth to address unexpected issues.

Courtroom Application

Practicing attorneys should note that this guide emphasizes federal court practice. State court practitioners must verify local rule variations, as evidence law can differ significantly between jurisdictions.

QUICK REFERENCE: MOST TESTED RULES

The following rules appear with disproportionate frequency on law school examinations and bar assessments. Mastery of these provisions should constitute your primary focus:

Critical Priority Rules

1. Rule 401-403 (Relevance and Prejudice): Foundation of all evidence analysis. Every evidence issue begins with relevance; Rule 403 balancing appears in virtually every examination.
2. Rule 404 (Character Evidence): Heavily tested prohibition with numerous exceptions. Pay particular attention to Rule 404(b) "other acts" evidence and the distinction between character and habit.

3. Rule 609 (Impeachment by Criminal Conviction): Complex balancing tests and time limitations. Know the differences between felony and misdemeanor convictions, and crimes of dishonesty.
4. Rules 801-807 (Hearsay): The most complex and heavily weighted topic. Master the definition, non-hearsay categories under 801(d), and major exceptions under 803 and 804.
5. Rule 803(1)-(2) (Present Sense Impression and Excited Utterance): Frequently tested hearsay exceptions with subtle but important distinctions.
6. Rule 803(6) (Business Records): Essential exception requiring careful attention to foundation requirements.

Secondary Priority Rules

1. Rule 702 (Expert Testimony): Increasingly important given the prevalence of expert witnesses. Understand Daubert reliability standards.
2. Rule 611 (Mode of Examination): Know the scope of cross-examination and leading question rules.
3. Rule 612 (Refreshing Recollection): Distinguish from recorded recollection under Rule 803(5).
4. Rules 901-902 (Authentication): Foundation requirements, particularly for electronic evidence and social media.
5. Rule 1002 (Best Evidence Rule): Know when original documents are required and recognized exceptions.

Examination Frequency Notes

1. Constitutional Integration: Be prepared to analyze Confrontation Clause issues alongside hearsay rules, particularly in criminal cases.
2. Policy Exclusions (Rules 407-411): While individually less complex, these rules appear regularly and often trap unwary students who confuse their scope and exceptions.
3. Privileges (Rule 501): Limited federal common law, but attorney-client privilege appears with sufficient frequency to warrant careful study.

Strategic Study Allocation

Given the typical weighting on examinations:

- Hearsay (40% of study time): Rules 801-807
- Relevance and Character (25% of study time): Rules 401-404, 412-415
- Witnesses and Impeachment (20% of study time): Rules 607-609, 611
- Authentication and Expert Testimony (10% of study time): Rules 701-702, 901-902
- Remaining Rules (5% of study time): Rules 407-411, 501, 1001-1008

This allocation reflects both examination frequency and the relative complexity of mastering each area. Adjust based on your professor's emphasis or jurisdiction-specific requirements.

FOUNDATIONS

WHAT ARE THE FEDERAL RULES OF EVIDENCE?

The Federal Rules of Evidence (FRE) are a comprehensive set of 67 rules that govern the admission and exclusion of evidence in federal courts throughout the United States. Adopted in 1975 after extensive study by legal scholars and practitioners, these rules replaced the previous common law system of evidence that varied significantly between jurisdictions.

Authority and Scope

The FRE derive their authority from the Rules Enabling Act, which grants the Supreme Court power to prescribe rules of practice and procedure for federal courts. These rules apply to:

- All federal district court proceedings (civil and criminal)
- Federal appellate court proceedings
- Supreme Court proceedings
- Certain federal administrative hearings

Important Limitation: The FRE do not apply to grand jury proceedings, sentencing hearings, preliminary hearings in criminal cases, or certain other specialized proceedings as specified in Rule 1101.

Historical Context

Before 1975, federal evidence law was a patchwork of common law principles, statutory provisions, and judicial decisions that varied significantly between circuits. The FRE created uniformity and predictability, establishing clear standards for evidence admissibility nationwide.

State Adoption

Most states have adopted evidence codes based on the Federal Rules, though significant variations exist. Practitioners must always verify local rules, as state evidence law can differ substantially from federal practice.

BASIC PRINCIPLES: RELEVANCE, RELIABILITY, FAIRNESS

Three fundamental principles underlie the Federal Rules of Evidence and guide all evidentiary decisions.

Relevance: The Foundation Principle

Core Concept: Evidence must have a logical connection to the facts that matter in the case.

Relevance serves as the primary gateway for evidence admission. Under Rule 401, evidence is relevant if it has "any tendency to make a fact more or less probable than it would be without the evidence" and that fact is "of consequence in determining the action."

Key Points:

- The standard is deliberately low - "any tendency" is sufficient
- Evidence need not prove a fact conclusively, only make it slightly more or less likely
- The fact must matter to the legal claims or defenses in the case

Example: In a negligence case, evidence that defendant was speeding is relevant because it makes careless driving more probable (logical relevance) and careless driving is an element of negligence (legal relevance).

Reliability: The Trustworthiness Principle

Core Concept: Evidence must be sufficiently trustworthy to warrant consideration by the factfinder.

Reliability concerns permeate the Federal Rules, appearing in various forms:

- Authentication requirements ensure evidence is what it purports to be
- Hearsay rules exclude unreliable out-of-court statements unless they fall within recognized exceptions

- Expert testimony standards require reliable methodologies and sufficient basis for opinions
- Original document requirements prefer the most reliable form of documentary evidence

Balancing Reliability and Practicality: The rules recognize that perfect reliability is impossible. Instead, they establish minimum thresholds that balance trustworthiness against practical necessity.

Fairness: The Due Process Principle

Core Concept: The evidence process must be fair to all parties and promote accurate factfinding.

Fairness manifests in several ways:

Procedural Fairness

- Advance notice requirements for certain types of evidence
- Opportunities to cross-examine witnesses
- Right to present contrary evidence

Substantive Fairness

- Rule 403 exclusion of unfairly prejudicial evidence
- Limitations on character evidence that might lead to improper inferences
- Protection of certain relationships through privilege rules

Systemic Fairness

- Uniform application of rules regardless of case type or party status
- Judicial discretion to ensure fair proceedings
- Appeal rights for evidentiary rulings

HOW TO ANALYZE EVIDENCE PROBLEMS

Effective evidence analysis requires a systematic approach. Use this framework for every evidence issue you encounter.

Step-by-Step Analysis Framework

Step 1: Identify the Evidence

- What specific item, statement, or testimony is being offered?
- Who is offering it and for what purpose?
- What fact is the proponent trying to prove or disprove?

Step 2: Relevance Analysis (Rules 401-402)

- Does the evidence make a fact more or less probable? (logical relevance)
- Is that fact of consequence to the case? (legal relevance)
- If not relevant, the analysis ends - evidence is inadmissible

Step 3: Check for Specific Exclusionary Rules

- Character evidence restrictions (Rule 404)

- Policy-based exclusions (Rules 407-411)
- Hearsay prohibitions (Rules 801-802)
- Authentication requirements (Rule 901)
- Best evidence rule (Rule 1002)
- Privilege protections (Rule 501)

Step 4: Rule 403 Balancing

- What is the probative value of the evidence?
- What are the potential dangers (unfair prejudice, confusion, delay)?
- Does the danger substantially outweigh the probative value?

Step 5: Consider Constitutional Issues

- Confrontation Clause concerns in criminal cases
- Due process implications
- Other constitutional protections

Common Analysis Mistakes

Mistake 1: Starting with Rule 403 instead of relevance

Correction: Always begin with Rules 401-402

Mistake 2: Confusing "prejudicial" with "unfairly prejudicial"

Correction: All adverse evidence is prejudicial; Rule 403 requires unfair prejudice

Mistake 3: Applying criminal rules to civil cases or vice versa

Correction: Note the procedural context and applicable standards

Mistake 4: Forgetting to consider the purpose for which evidence is offered

Correction: The same evidence may be admissible for one purpose but not another

MAKING AND RESPONDING TO OBJECTIONS

Effective objection practice is essential for controlling the evidence that reaches the jury. Master these fundamental skills for courtroom success.

Types of Objections

Relevance Objections:

- "Objection, Your Honor. Irrelevant."
- "Objection. The probative value is substantially outweighed by unfair prejudice under Rule 403."

Foundation Objections:

- "Objection. Lack of foundation."
- "Objection. Improper authentication."

Hearsay Objections:

- "Objection. Hearsay."
- "Objection. Hearsay not within any recognized exception."

Form Objections:

- "Objection. Leading." (on direct examination)
- "Objection. Calls for speculation."
- "Objection. Compound question."

Timing and Preservation

General Rule: Objections must be made when the question is asked, not after the answer is given.

Exception: Motion to strike when an objection could not reasonably have been made before the answer.

Preservation Requirements:

- State the specific ground for objection
- Make the objection at the first opportunity
- Obtain a ruling from the court
- If overruled, make an offer of proof to preserve appellate rights

Strategic Considerations

When to Object:

- The evidence is clearly inadmissible and harmful

- You can reasonably expect to win the objection
- The objection won't highlight damaging evidence

When NOT to Object:

- The evidence is marginally harmful and the objection might be overruled
- Objecting would emphasize unfavorable evidence
- The objection would disrupt your cross-examination rhythm

Responding to Objections

If Your Question is Objected To:

- Listen to the objection and ruling
- Rephrase the question to cure any defect
- If sustained, move to a different topic or lay additional foundation

If Evidence is Excluded:

- Make an offer of proof outside the jury's presence
- Preserve the record for appeal
- Consider alternative ways to present the same information

Foundation Requirements

1. Personal Knowledge: Witness must have firsthand knowledge of the facts they're testifying about.

2. Authentication: Documents and physical evidence must be shown to be what they purport to be.
3. Chain of Custody: For physical evidence, establish continuous possession from collection to trial.
4. Business Records: Must show regular business practice, contemporaneous recording, and reliable source of information.
5. Expert Testimony: Must establish witness qualifications and reliable basis for opinions.

Practice Tips

1. Be Specific: "Objection, hearsay" is better than "Objection."
2. Stay Professional: Never argue with the judge or opposing counsel during objections.
3. Know Your Judge: Some judges prefer detailed arguments; others want brief statements.
4. Prepare Key Objections: Anticipate likely evidentiary disputes and prepare concise arguments.
5. Use Limiting Instructions: When evidence is admissible for one purpose but not another, request appropriate jury instructions.

Article I – General Provisions

RULE 101. SCOPE AND DEFINITIONS

These foundational rules establish how all other evidence rules operate in practice. Rule 103 governs the critical process of making and responding to objections, which is essential for preserving issues for appeal. Rule 104 addresses preliminary questions and conditional admissibility determinations. These procedural rules form the framework for resolving evidence disputes.

(a) Scope

These rules apply to proceedings in United States courts. The specific courts and proceedings to which the rules apply, along with exceptions, are set out in Rule 1101.

(b) Definitions

In these rules:

- "civil case" means a civil action or proceeding;
- "criminal case" includes a criminal proceeding;
- "public office" includes a public agency;
- "record" includes a memorandum, report, or data compilation;

- "rule prescribed by the Supreme Court" means a rule adopted by the Supreme Court under statutory authority; and
- "a reference to any kind of written material or any other medium includes electronically stored information."

Key Points:

- These definitions apply throughout all Federal Rules of Evidence
- The electronic information definition (added in 2011) reflects modern technology
- "Record" is broadly defined to include various forms of data storage
- The scope is limited to federal courts - state courts may have different rules

RULE 102. PURPOSE

These rules should be construed so as to administer every proceeding fairly, eliminate unjustifiable expense and delay, and promote the development of evidence law to the end of ascertaining the truth and securing a just determination.

Analysis:

Rule 102 establishes the overarching goals that guide interpretation of all evidence rules:

Primary Goals:

- Fair administration of proceedings
- Efficiency - eliminate unnecessary expense and delay

- Truth-seeking - ascertain facts accurately
- Justice - secure just determinations

Practical Impact:

- Courts use these principles when interpreting ambiguous rules
- Judges have discretion to manage proceedings efficiently
- The rule emphasizes substance over technicalities
- Truth-seeking takes precedence over rigid rule application

Exam Alert: Rule 102 rarely appears as a standalone issue but influences how courts apply other evidence rules. When rules seem to conflict or are ambiguous, courts look to these underlying principles.

RULE 103. RULINGS ON EVIDENCE

A. Preserving a Claim of Error

A party may claim error in a ruling to admit or exclude evidence only if the error affects a substantial right of the party and:

(1) if the ruling admits evidence, a party, on the record:

a) timely objects or moves to strike; and
b) states the specific ground, unless it was apparent from the context; or

(2) if the ruling excludes evidence, a party informs the court of its substance by an offer of proof, unless the substance was apparent from the context.

B. Not Needing to Renew an Objection or Offer of Proof

Once the court rules definitively on the record—either before or at trial—a party need not renew an objection or offer of proof to preserve a claim of error for appeal.

C. Court's Statement About the Ruling; Directing an Offer of Proof

The court may make any statement about the character or form of the evidence, the objection made, and the ruling. The court may direct that an offer of proof be made in question-and-answer form.

D. Preventing the Jury from Hearing Inadmissible Evidence

To the extent practicable, the court must conduct a jury trial so that inadmissible evidence is not suggested to the jury by any means.

E. Taking Notice of Plain Error

A court may take notice of a plain error affecting a substantial right, even if the claim of error was not properly preserved.

Critical Practice Points

Preserving Error for Appeal:

- Timeliness: Object when the question is asked, not after the answer
- Specificity: State the exact ground for objection ("Objection, hearsay" not just "Objection")
- Offer of Proof: When evidence is excluded, make a record of what you would have proven

Common Mistakes:

- General objections: "Objection" without stating grounds
- Late objections: Waiting until after the damaging answer
- Failing to make offers of proof: Losing appellate rights by not preserving excluded evidence

Strategic Considerations:

- Definitive rulings: Once a judge rules definitively (often in pretrial motions), you don't need to re-object at trial
- Plain error: Even if you fail to object, egregious errors affecting substantial rights may still be reviewable
- Jury management: Courts should prevent inadmissible evidence from reaching the jury

Practice Examples

Proper Objection:

"Objection, Your Honor. The question calls for hearsay not within any recognized exception."

Proper Offer of Proof:

"Your Honor, if permitted to testify, the witness would state that the defendant admitted fault at the scene, which is relevant to the issue of liability."

RULE 104. PRELIMINARY QUESTIONS

A. In General

The court must decide any preliminary question about whether a witness is qualified, a privilege exists, or evidence is admissible. In so deciding, the court is not bound by evidence rules, except those on privilege.

B. Relevance That Depends on a Fact

When the relevance of evidence depends on whether a fact exists, proof must be introduced sufficient to support a finding that the fact does exist.

C. Conducting a Hearing So That the Jury Cannot Hear It

The court must conduct any hearing on a preliminary question so that the jury cannot hear it if:

(1) the hearing involves the admissibility of a confession in a criminal case;

(2) a defendant in a criminal case is a witness and so requests; or

(3) justice so requires.

D. Cross-Examining a Defendant in a Criminal Case

By testifying on a preliminary question, a defendant in a criminal case does not become subject to cross-examination on other issues in the case.

Key Concepts

Judge vs. Jury Roles:

- Judge decides: Whether evidence rules are satisfied (admissibility)
- Jury decides: What weight to give admitted evidence (credibility and persuasiveness)

Preliminary Fact Standards

Rule 104(a) - Judge decides by preponderance:

- Witness qualifications
- Privilege claims
- Authentication
- Hearsay exception requirements
- Expert testimony reliability

Rule 104(b) - Jury decides sufficiency:

- Conditional relevance situations
- Judge only requires sufficient evidence to support a jury finding
- Lower standard than 104(a)

Example of 104(b): Plaintiff claims defendant made an admission. The judge doesn't decide whether defendant actually made the statement (that's for the jury), only whether there's sufficient evidence that a reasonable jury could find the statement was made.

Criminal Case Protections

- Confession hearings must be outside jury presence
- Defendant can request private hearings on preliminary questions
- Testifying on admissibility doesn't open the defendant to general cross-examination

Practical Applications

- Authentication disputes: Judge decides if there's sufficient evidence the document is genuine
- Hearsay exceptions: Judge decides if exception requirements are met\Expert qualifications: Judge decides if witness has sufficient expertise

RULE 105. LIMITED ADMISSIBILITY

If the court admits evidence that is admissible for one purpose or against one party but not for another purpose or against another party, the court, on timely request, must restrict the evidence to its proper scope and instruct the jury accordingly.

Core Concept: Evidence may be admissible for some purposes but not others. When this occurs, the court must give limiting instructions to prevent improper use.

Common Scenarios

Prior Crimes Evidence (Rule 404(b)):

- Admissible to show motive, but not to prove bad character
- Limiting instruction: "You may consider this evidence only on the question of motive, not to conclude that defendant is a bad person likely to commit crimes"

Settlement Evidence (Rule 408):

- Inadmissible to prove liability, but may be admissible to impeach witness
- Limiting instruction required to prevent improper inference

Hearsay Statements:

- May be admissible against one party but not another
- Co-conspirator statements admissible only against parties to the conspiracy

Practice Requirements:

- Timely request: Must ask for limiting instruction promptly
- Specific instruction: Court should tailor instruction to the particular evidence and purpose

- Strategic decision: Consider whether limiting instruction draws more attention to harmful evidence

Effectiveness Question: Legal scholars debate whether limiting instructions actually work or whether they're "like telling someone not to think of a pink elephant." However, they remain a fundamental protection in evidence law.

RULE 106. REMAINDER OF OR RELATED WRITINGS OR RECORDED STATEMENTS

If a party introduces all or part of a writing or recorded statement, an adverse party may require the introduction, at that time, of any other part—or any other writing or recorded statement—that in fairness ought to be considered at the same time.

Purpose: Prevent misleading impressions from partial quotations or selective presentation of written or recorded material.

Key Requirements:

- Fairness standard: The additional material must be necessary for fair understanding
- Contemporaneous introduction: The completing evidence comes in immediately, not later in trial
- Related material: Must be from the same writing/recording or a closely related one

Common Applications

Partial Letter: If one party introduces favorable portions of a letter, the opponent can require introduction of the complete letter or related correspondence.

Recorded Conversations: If part of a phone call or meeting recording is played, the opponent may require playing additional portions that provide necessary context.

Email Chains: Introduction of one email may require production of related emails in the same chain for context.

Strategic Considerations:

- For the proponent: Consider whether introducing partial evidence will backfire by allowing opponent to introduce harmful context
- For the opponent: Determine whether the completing evidence helps your case or merely provides neutral context
- Timing: This rule allows immediate introduction, disrupting the proponent's presentation strategy

Relationship to Other Rules: Rule 106 can override other exclusionary rules when necessary for fairness, though courts apply this exception cautiously

Practical Tip: When planning to use excerpts from documents or recordings, anticipate what additional material your opponent might introduce under Rule 106 and prepare accordingly.

ARTICLE II – JUDICIAL NOTICE

Courts may accept certain indisputable facts as true without requiring formal proof from the parties. Rule 201 allows judicial notice of adjudicative facts that are generally known in the community or capable of accurate determination from reliable sources. This efficiency mechanism saves time on matters like historical dates, geographic facts, or established scientific principles.

RULE 201. JUDICIAL NOTICE OF ADJUDICATIVE FACTS

Core Concept: Courts may accept certain obvious facts as true without requiring formal proof.

Two Types of Facts Subject to Judicial Notice:

1. Generally known facts within the court's jurisdiction

2. Readily determinable facts from reliable sources

Examples:

- Calendar dates ("January 1, 2025 was a Wednesday")
- Geographic facts ("Boston is north of New York")
- Exchange rates from official sources

- Weather from government records

Key Procedural Points

- Court may notice on its own or must notice when properly requested
- Parties have right to be heard on propriety of taking notice
- Can occur at any stage of proceedings

Critical Distinction - Jury Instructions

- Civil cases: Jury must accept noticed fact as conclusive
- Criminal cases: Jury may accept noticed fact but is not required to

What Cannot Be Noticed

- Disputed material facts central to the case
- Complex matters requiring expert interpretation

Article III – Presumptions

These rules govern legal presumptions in civil cases—rebuttable assumptions that shift the burden of producing evidence to the opposing party. Rule 301 establishes the federal "bursting bubble" approach where presumptions disappear once contradicted by evidence. Rule 302 requires applying state presumption law in diversity jurisdiction cases, respecting federalism principles.

RULE 301. PRESUMPTIONS IN CIVIL CASES

Core Concept: When certain basic facts (predicate facts) are proven, the law requires assuming another fact (presumed fact) exists unless the opponent rebuts it.

The "Bursting Bubble" Approach

1. Proponent proves predicate facts → presumption arises

2. Opponent must produce evidence challenging presumed fact

3. If opponent produces sufficient rebuttal evidence → presumption disappears

4. Important: Only shifts burden of production, NOT burden of persuasion

Common Presumptions

- Mail delivery: Properly mailed letter presumed received
- Death: Person missing 7+ years presumed dead
- Legitimacy: Child born during marriage presumed legitimate
- Official regularity: Government officials presumed to perform duties properly

RULE 302. APPLYING STATE LAW IN CIVIL CASES

In federal court hearing state law claims, state law governs the effect of presumptions.

Why This Matters

- Many states use different approaches than federal "bursting bubble"
- Some states shift burden of persuasion, not just production
- Critical in diversity jurisdiction cases

Quick Review Points

Judicial Notice (Rule 201):

- Only for facts "not subject to reasonable dispute"
- Different jury instructions in civil vs. criminal cases
- Saves time by eliminating proof of obvious facts

Presumptions (Rules 301-302):

- Federal rule: shifts production burden only ("bursting bubble")
- State law governs in diversity cases
- Presumptions can disappear but underlying evidence remains

Exam Tips:

- These rules rarely appear as major issues
- More likely to see in multiple-choice questions
- Focus on civil/criminal distinction for judicial notice
- Remember burden shifting concepts for presumptions

Article IV – Relevance

Relevance serves as the fundamental gateway to admissibility, evidence must be relevant to be considered for admission. Rules 401-403 establish basic relevance standards and the crucial balancing test against unfair prejudice. Rules 404-415 address character evidence limitations and specific policy-based exclusions like subsequent remedial measures and settlement negotiations.

This article contains some of the most frequently tested rules in evidence law. Master these concepts for exam success and effective practice.

RULE 401. TEST FOR RELEVANT EVIDENCE

Evidence is relevant if:

(a) it has any tendency to make a fact more or less probable than it would be without the evidence; and

(b) the fact is of consequence in determining the action.

Understanding Relevance

Two-Part Test:

1. Logical Relevance ("any tendency")

- Does the evidence make any material fact more or less likely?
- Standard is extremely low - "any tendency" is sufficient
- Courts use "brick is not wall" metaphor - even small pieces of evidence can be relevant

2. Legal Relevance ("of consequence")

- Must relate to a fact that matters to the case
- Tied to elements of claims, defenses, or credibility
- Consider pleadings, applicable law, and case theory

Key Principles:

- Inclusive Standard: The bar for relevance is intentionally low. Evidence doesn't need to be highly probative or conclusive - just having "any tendency" to make a fact more or less probable is sufficient.
- Direct vs. Circumstantial Evidence: Both can be relevant. Circumstantial evidence that supports reasonable inferences is relevant even if it doesn't directly prove the point.
- Chain of Inferences: Evidence may be relevant through multiple logical steps, as long as each step is reasonable.

Common Relevance Issues

Temporal Proximity:

- Events close in time to the incident are generally more relevant

- Remote events may still be relevant if logically connected
- Consider alternative causes and changed conditions

Character for Truthfulness:

- Evidence of witness's character for honesty is relevant to credibility
- Prior consistent/inconsistent statements are relevant to truthfulness

Motive and Intent:

- Evidence showing why someone acted is highly relevant
- Financial pressures, personal relationships, business interests
- Prior similar acts may show motive or intent

Physical Evidence:

- Photographs relevant if they fairly represent scene/object
- Demonstrative evidence relevant if it aids understanding
- Scientific evidence relevant if methodology is sound

Exam Strategy for Rule 401

Analysis Framework:

1. Identify the material fact at issue

2. Explain how the evidence makes that fact more/less probable

3. Confirm the fact is "of consequence" to the case

4. Apply the low standard - argue both sides

Common Mistakes:

- Setting the bar too high - remember "any tendency" standard
- Failing to identify the specific material fact
- Confusing relevance with admissibility (relevance is just the first step)

RULE 402. GENERAL ADMISSIBILITY OF RELEVANT EVIDENCE

Relevant evidence is admissible unless any of the following provides otherwise:

- the United States Constitution;
- a federal statute;
- these rules; or
- other rules prescribed by the Supreme Court.

Irrelevant evidence is not admissible.

The General Rule of Inclusion

Default Position: All relevant evidence is admissible unless specifically excluded by:

- Constitutional provisions (due process, confrontation clause, etc.)

- Federal statutes
- Federal Rules of Evidence
- Other Supreme Court rules

Practical Impact: Rule 402 establishes that relevance alone is usually sufficient for admissibility. The burden is on the opponent to show why relevant evidence should be excluded.

Irrelevant Evidence: Absolutely inadmissible - no exceptions, no judicial discretion.

RULE 403. EXCLUDING RELEVANT EVIDENCE FOR PREJUDICE, CONFUSION, OR OTHER REASONS

The court may exclude relevant evidence if its probative value is substantially outweighed by a danger of one or more of the following: unfair prejudice, confusing the issues, misleading the jury, undue delay, wasting time, or needlessly presenting cumulative evidence.

The Balancing Test

Standard: "Substantially outweighed" - this is a high bar favoring admission.

Six Grounds for Exclusion:

1. Unfair Prejudice

   - Evidence that appeals to emotion rather than logic
   - Risk jury will give evidence undue weight

- "Unfair" is key - all evidence is somewhat prejudicial to someone
- Examples: Gruesome photos, inflammatory language, appeals to bias

2. Confusing the Issues

- Evidence that obscures or complicates the main issues
- Side issues that distract from central questions
- Complex technical evidence that overwhelms lay jury

3. Misleading the Jury

- Evidence that creates false impressions
- Statistics taken out of context
- Demonstrations that don't accurately reflect real conditions

4. Undue Delay

- Evidence that requires excessive time to present
- Disproportionate to its probative value
- Consider court calendar and trial efficiency

5. Waste of Time

- Cumulative evidence that adds little new information
- Repetitive testimony on established points
- Evidence that belabors obvious facts

6. Needlessly Cumulative

- Multiple witnesses saying the same thing
- Excessive documentation of undisputed facts
- Redundant expert testimony

Balancing Analysis Framework

Step 1: Assess Probative Value

- How strongly does evidence support/refute material fact?
- Is there alternative evidence available?
- How central is the fact to the case?

Step 2: Identify Specific Dangers

- Which Rule 403 factors apply?
- How serious is the risk?
- Can limiting instructions or other measures reduce danger?

Step 3: Apply "Substantially Outweighed" Standard

- Strong presumption in favor of admission
- Exclusion is extraordinary remedy
- Consider alternatives (limiting instructions, redaction, etc.)

Strategic Considerations

For Proponents:

- Lead with probative value arguments
- Offer limiting instructions or stipulations
- Propose alternatives (redacted versions, summaries)
- Address timing and efficiency concerns

For Opponents:

- Focus on specific Rule 403 dangers
- Quantify time/confusion costs
- Suggest alternative evidence is available
- Propose less prejudicial alternatives

Common Applications

Gruesome Photos:

- High prejudicial impact vs. probative value on cause of death
- Often admitted with limiting instructions
- Consider whether medical examiner testimony sufficient

Prior Bad Acts:

- Risk of character propensity reasoning
- Must have clear non-character purpose
- Limiting instructions usually required

Demonstrative Evidence:

- Computer animations, day-in-the-life videos
- Risk of misleading if not accurate recreation
- Consider whether live testimony sufficient

Settlement/Insurance Evidence:

- High prejudice risk if admitted for improper purpose
- Usually excluded under specific rules (407-411)
- Rule 403 provides backup exclusion

RULE 404. CHARACTER EVIDENCE; CRIMES OR OTHER ACTS

A. Character Evidence

(1) Prohibited Uses. Evidence of a person's character or character trait is not admissible to prove that on a particular occasion the person acted in accordance with the character or trait.

(2) Exceptions for a Defendant or Victim in a Criminal Case:

(a) a defendant may offer evidence of the defendant's pertinent character trait, and if the evidence is admitted, the prosecutor may offer evidence to rebut it;

(b) subject to the limitations in Rule 412, a defendant may offer evidence of an alleged victim's pertinent character trait, and if the evidence is admitted, the prosecutor may:

(i) offer evidence to rebut it; and

(ii) offer evidence of the defendant's same character trait; and

(C) in a homicide case, the prosecutor may offer evidence of the alleged victim's trait for peacefulness to rebut evidence that the victim was the first aggressor.

(3) Exceptions for a Witness. Evidence of a witness's character for truthfulness or untruthfulness is admissible under Rules 607, 608, and 609.

B. Crimes, Wrongs, or Other Acts

(1) Prohibited Purpose. Evidence of a crime, wrong, or other act is not admissible to prove a person's character in order to show that on a particular occasion the person acted in accordance with the character.

(2) Permitted Purposes. This evidence may be admissible for another purpose, such as proving motive, opportunity, intent, preparation, plan, knowledge, identity, absence of mistake, or lack of accident.

(3) Notice in a Criminal Case. In a criminal case, the prosecutor must provide reasonable notice in advance of trial, or during trial if the court excuses lack of pretrial notice, of the general nature of any such evidence that the prosecutor intends to use.

Understanding Character Evidence

The General Prohibition

Core Principle: Cannot use character evidence to prove someone acted "in character" on a particular occasion.

Rationale:

- Risk of unfair prejudice
- Encourage focus on specific conduct, not general character
- Avoid trials becoming character assassination
- People can act out of character

The Propensity Box: Think of character evidence as having a "propensity box" around it. Evidence is inadmissible if it goes through this box (proving character to show conduct).

Rule 404(A) - Character of Parties

Civil Cases: Character evidence generally inadmissible except:

- When character is directly in issue (defamation, negligent entrustment, child custody)
- Witness credibility (Rule 608)

Criminal Cases - Three Exceptions:

Exception 1: Defendant's Character

- Defendant may "open the door" by offering evidence of pertinent good character
- Must be pertinent to the crime charged
- If defendant opens door, prosecution may rebut with bad character evidence
- Strategic decision - opening door allows prosecution response

Exception 2: Victim's Character

- Defendant may offer evidence of victim's pertinent character trait
- Common in self-defense cases (victim's violence)
- Subject to Rule 412 limitations in sexual assault cases

If defendant opens door, prosecution may:

- Rebut victim's bad character, AND

- Offer evidence of defendant's same bad trait

Exception 3: Homicide Cases - Victim's Peacefulness

- Prosecution may offer evidence of victim's peaceful character
- Only to rebut evidence that victim was first aggressor
- Does not require defendant to first introduce victim's character

Rule 404(b) - Prior Bad Acts Evidence

The MIMIC Rule: Evidence of other crimes/wrongs admissible for non-character purposes:

M - Motive: Why defendant acted

I - Intent: Defendant's state of mind

M - Mistake (absence of): Shows conduct was deliberate

I - Identity: Signature crime or distinctive method

C - Common plan/scheme: Pattern of behavior

Plus: Knowledge, opportunity, preparation, lack of accident

Analysis Framework for Rule 404(b)

Step 1: Identify the Non-Character Purpose

- Must be specific and material to the case
- Cannot be mere pretext for character evidence
- Consider elements of charged offense

Step 2: Assess Probative Value

- How strong is the connection to the non-character purpose?
- How similar are the prior acts?
- How close in time?

Step 3: Rule 403 Balancing

- High risk of unfair prejudice with prior bad acts
- Limiting instructions may help but have limited effectiveness
- Consider strength of other evidence on the point

Step 4: Notice Requirement (Criminal Cases)

- Prosecution must provide pretrial notice
- Include general nature of evidence and purpose
- Court may excuse lack of notice for good cause

Common 404(b) Applications

Motive Examples:

- Prior threats showing why defendant harmed victim
- Financial difficulties showing motive for fraud
- Romantic relationships showing motive for jealousy crimes

Intent Examples:

- Prior similar fraudulent schemes showing intent to defraud
- Pattern of domestic violence showing intent to harm

- Drug dealer's prior sales showing intent to distribute

Identity Examples:

- Distinctive signature or method of operation
- Unique physical evidence linking crimes
- Pattern so distinctive it identifies perpetrator

Knowledge Examples:

- Prior drug transactions showing knowledge of narcotics
- Experience with weapons showing knowledge of danger
- Prior complaints showing knowledge of defective condition

Common Plan Examples:

- Series of similar fraudulent schemes
- Pattern of abuse escalating to murder
- Coordinated criminal enterprise

Strategic Considerations

For Prosecutors:

- Provide clear notice and specific non-character purpose
- Consider timing - pretrial motions vs. trial objections
- Prepare limiting instructions
- Ensure sufficient similarity between acts

For Defense:

- Challenge the stated non-character purpose
- Argue insufficient similarity or temporal remoteness

- Emphasize Rule 403 prejudice
- Request detailed limiting instructions

For Civil Practitioners:

- Remember Rule 404 applies in civil cases too
- Consider when character is directly in issue
- Use Rule 404(b) for non-character purposes in appropriate cases

Exam Tips for Rule 404

Issue Spotting:

- Look for evidence of defendant's prior crimes or bad acts
- Identify whether evidence is offered for character or non-character purpose
- Consider victim character evidence in criminal cases
- Watch for "opening the door" scenarios

Analysis Structure:

1. Is this character evidence or specific act evidence?

2. If character evidence, does an exception apply?

3. If specific act evidence, what is the non-character purpose?

4. Does the evidence satisfy Rule 403 balancing?

5. Are procedural requirements (notice) satisfied?

RULE 405. METHODS OF PROVING CHARACTER

A. By Reputation or Opinion

When evidence of a person's character or character trait is admissible, it may be proved by testimony about the person's reputation or by testimony in the form of an opinion. On cross-examination of the character witness, the court may allow an inquiry into relevant specific instances of the person's conduct.

B. By Specific Instances of Conduct

When a person's character or character trait is an essential element of a charge, claim, or defense, it may also be proved by relevant specific instances of the person's conduct.

How to Prove Character

Method 1: Reputation Evidence (Permitted)

What it is: Testimony about what the community says about the person's character.

Foundation Requirements:

- Witness must be familiar with person's reputation
- In relevant community (neighborhood, workplace, etc.)
- At relevant time period
- For the specific character trait at issue

Example: "In our neighborhood, John has a reputation for being honest and law-abiding."

Cross-Examination: Opponent may ask "Have you heard" questions about specific bad acts to test knowledge of reputation.

Method 2: Opinion Evidence (Permitted)

What it is: Witness's personal opinion about the person's character based on personal knowledge.

Foundation Requirements:

- Witness must know the person well enough to form opinion
- Opinion must be based on adequate personal observation
- Must specify the character trait
- Cannot give specific examples on direct examination

Example: "Based on my 10-year friendship with John, I believe he is an honest person."

Cross-Examination: Opponent may ask "Did you know" questions about specific bad acts to test basis of opinion.

Method 3: Specific Acts (Limited Situations)

When Allowed: Only when character is an "essential element" of the case.

Essential Element Cases:

- Defamation (truth defense requires proving victim's bad character)

- Negligent entrustment (owner's knowledge of driver's incompetence)
- Child custody (parent's fitness)
- Self-defense (knowledge of victim's violent character)
- Entrapment (defendant's predisposition)

What it means: The law itself makes character a required element to prove or disprove.

Cross-Examination of Character Witnesses

"Have You Heard" Questions (Reputation Witnesses):

- Tests witness's knowledge of community reputation
- "Have you heard that John was arrested for embezzlement last year?"
- Must have good faith basis for question
- Answer doesn't prove the underlying act occurred

"Did You Know" Questions (Opinion Witnesses):

- Tests adequacy of witness's personal knowledge
- "Did you know that John was convicted of fraud in 2020?"
- Must have good faith basis for question
- Answer doesn't prove the underlying act occurred

Strategic Considerations

- Character witness opens door to damaging cross-examination

- Consider whether character evidence is worth the risk
- Prepare witnesses for potential specific act questions
- Have good faith basis for all cross-examination questions

RULE 406. HABIT; ROUTINE PRACTICE

Evidence of a person's habit or an organization's routine practice may be admitted to prove that on a particular occasion the person or organization acted in accordance with the habit or routine practice. The court may admit this evidence regardless of whether it is corroborated or whether there was an eyewitness.

Habit vs. Character - Critical Distinction

Requirements for Habit:

- Specific conduct: Detailed, particular behavior
- Regular response: To specific circumstances
- Automatic/semi-automatic: Little conscious thought required
- Frequency: Repeated many times in similar situations

Examples of Proper Habit Evidence:

- Always stopping at particular stop sign on route to work
- Invariably locking office door when leaving
- Routine practice of checking equipment before each use

- Regular custom of mailing bills on specific day each month

Habit vs. Character Comparison

Habit (Admissible):

- Specific, detailed conduct
- Automatic response to particular situation
- High degree of regularity
- Predicts specific behavior

Character (Generally Inadmissible):

- General disposition or personality trait
- Broad behavioral tendencies
- Lower predictive value
- Describes general nature

Example Distinctions:

- Habit: "John always locks his car when parking at the mall"
- Character: "John is a careful person"
- Habit: "Dr. Smith invariably sterilizes instruments before surgery"
- Character: "Dr. Smith is conscientious about patient safety"

Organizational Routine Practice

Business Organizations: May establish routine practices that predict behavior:

- Standard operating procedures
- Regular business customs
- Institutional practices with high regularity

Foundation Requirements:

- Witness with knowledge of organization's practices
- Evidence of regularity and specificity
- Testimony that practice was in effect at relevant time

Examples:

- Bank's routine practice for processing deposits
- Hospital's standard procedure for patient intake
- Company's regular custom for equipment maintenance

Admissibility Standards

1. No Corroboration Required: Unlike some character evidence, habit evidence doesn't need independent confirmation.
2. No Eyewitness Required: Can prove habit even without witnesses to the specific occasion.
3. Judicial Discretion: Courts have flexibility in determining whether evidence qualifies as habit vs. character.

Strategic Uses

Civil Cases:

- Negligence cases: routine safety practices
- Contract disputes: regular business customs
- Product liability: standard manufacturing procedures

Criminal Cases:

- Less common but available
- Defendant's regular habits may support alibi
- Victim's routine practices may be relevant

Practice Tips:

- Develop detailed testimony about specific practices
- Emphasize regularity and automaticity
- Distinguish from general character traits
- Consider Rule 403 balancing for prejudicial habits

RULE 407. SUBSEQUENT REMEDIAL MEASURES

When measures are taken that would have made an earlier injury or harm less likely to occur, evidence of the subsequent measures is not admissible to prove:

- negligence;
- culpable conduct;
- a defect in a product or its design; or
- a need for a warning or instruction.

But the court may admit this evidence for another purpose, such as impeachment or—if disputed—proving ownership, control, or the feasibility of precautionary measures.

Understanding Subsequent Remedial Measures

Policy Rationale: Encourage people to fix dangerous conditions without fear that repairs will be used against them in litigation.

Scope of Protection:

- Physical repairs and modifications
- Changes in procedures or policies
- Installation of safety equipment
- Additional warnings or instructions
- Design changes to products

Timing: Must occur after the injury/harm that forms basis of lawsuit.

Prohibited Uses

Cannot Prove:

- Negligence: That defendant was careless
- Culpable conduct: Fault or wrongdoing
- Product defect: Flaw in design or manufacture
- Need for warning: Inadequate instructions

Example: After slip-and-fall accident, store installs warning signs. Cannot use signs to prove store was negligent in not having them originally.

Permitted Uses

May Prove:

- Impeachment: Contradict witness testimony
- Ownership: Who controlled premises
- Control: Authority over condition
- Feasibility: Whether safety measures were possible

Common Example - Feasibility: Defendant claims safety measure was impossible/impractical. Subsequent implementation proves feasibility.

Impeachment Example: Witness testifies "there was no way to make it safer." Subsequent safety measures contradict this testimony.

Practical Applications

Requirements for Exclusion:

- Measure must be "subsequent" to the harm
- Measure must be "remedial" (make future harm less likely)
- Must be offered for prohibited purpose

Strategic Considerations:

- Plaintiff: Find alternative theories for admissibility
- Defendant: Consider timing of repairs and potential admissible purposes
- Both: Understand scope of protection and exceptions

RULE 408. COMPROMISE OFFERS AND NEGOTIATIONS

A. Prohibited Uses

Evidence of the following is not admissible—on behalf of any party—either to prove or disprove the validity or amount of a disputed claim or to impeach by a prior inconsistent statement or a contradiction:

(1) furnishing, promising, or offering—or accepting, promising to accept, or offering to accept—a valuable consideration in compromising or attempting to compromise the claim; and

(2) conduct or a statement made during compromise negotiations about the claim—except when offered in a criminal case and when the negotiations related to a claim by a public office in the exercise of its regulatory, investigative, or enforcement authority.

B. Exceptions

The court may admit this evidence for another purpose, such as proving a witness's bias or prejudice, negating a contention of undue delay, or proving an effort to obstruct a criminal investigation or prosecution.

Settlement Negotiations Protection

Policy Rationale: Encourage settlement by protecting confidentiality of compromise discussions.

Scope of Protection:

- Settlement offers and acceptances
- Statements made during negotiations
- Valuable consideration offered/accepted
- Conduct during settlement discussions

Requirements for Protection:

- Must be an actual "dispute" over validity or amount
- Must be genuine settlement negotiations
- Applies to all parties, even non-participants

What's Protected

Offers of Compromise:

- "We'll pay $10,000 to settle"
- "How about we split the difference"
- Offers to accept reduced amounts

Settlement Negotiations:

- Factual admissions during discussions
- Legal arguments about case strength
- Strategic discussions about resolution

Conduct During Negotiations:

- Payment of settlement amounts

- Execution of settlement agreements
- Participation in mediation

Key Limitations

Dispute Requirement: No protection for undisputed claims.

- "I owe you $1000 and here's $800" (no dispute = no protection)
- "I disagree that I owe anything, but I'll pay $500 to settle" (disputed = protected)

Criminal Case Exception: Limited protection in criminal cases when government exercising regulatory authority.

Pre-Existing Evidence: Rule doesn't protect evidence that exists independently of settlement negotiations.

Permitted Uses

Bias/Prejudice: Show witness has financial interest in outcome.

Undue Delay: Counter claims of foot-dragging.

Obstruction: Evidence of attempting to interfere with investigation.

Other Civil Cases: Settlement with one party may be admissible in suit against different party.

Strategic Considerations

Creating Protected Environment:

- Use clear settlement language ("This is a settlement offer")
- Reference Rule 408 protection explicitly
- Document disputed nature of claim
- Consider mediation for additional protection

Avoiding Waiver:

- Don't reference settlement discussions in pleadings
- Be careful about partial disclosures
- Understand scope of protection

RULE 409. OFFERS TO PAY MEDICAL AND SIMILAR EXPENSES

Evidence of furnishing, promising to pay, or offering to pay medical, hospital, or similar expenses resulting from an injury is not admissible to prove liability for the injury.

Medical Expense Payments

Policy Rationale: Encourage humanitarian assistance without legal consequences.

Scope:

- Medical expenses
- Hospital bills

- Similar injury-related expenses
- Promises to pay such expenses

Key Limitation: Only the payment/offer is protected, NOT accompanying statements.

Example:

- Protected: "I'll pay your medical bills"
- Not Protected: "I'll pay your medical bills because this was all my fault"

Contrast with Rule 408: Much narrower protection than settlement negotiations.

RULE 410. PLEAS, PLEA DISCUSSIONS, AND RELATED STATEMENTS

A. Prohibited Uses

In a civil or criminal case, evidence of the following is not admissible against the defendant who made the plea or participated in the plea discussions:

(1) a guilty plea that was later withdrawn;

(2) a nolo contendere plea;

(3) a statement made during a proceeding on either of those pleas under Federal Rule of Criminal Procedure 11; and

(4) a statement made during plea discussions with an attorney for the prosecuting authority if the discussions did not result in a guilty plea or resulted in a later-withdrawn guilty plea.

B. Exceptions

The court may admit a statement described in Rule 410(a)(3) or (4):

(1) in any proceeding in which another statement made during the same plea or plea discussions has been introduced, if in fairness the statements ought to be considered together; or

(2) in a criminal proceeding for perjury or false statement, if the defendant made the statement under oath, on the record, and with counsel present.

Plea Negotiation Protection

Policy Rationale: Encourage plea negotiations by protecting statements from later use.

Protected Categories:

1. Withdrawn Guilty Pleas

- Pleas entered but later withdrawn by court permission
- Cannot be used against defendant in any subsequent proceeding

2. Nolo Contendere Pleas

- "No contest" pleas
- Cannot be used in civil or criminal proceedings

3. Rule 11 Proceeding Statements

- Statements during plea colloquy
- Judge's questioning about factual basis for plea

4. Plea Discussion Statements

- Must be with prosecuting authority or agents
- Must be during actual plea negotiations
- No protection if discussions resulted in plea that wasn't withdrawn

Limitations and Exceptions

1. **Scope:** Protection only applies against the defendant who made statements.
2. **Completeness:** If defendant introduces part of plea discussions, prosecution may introduce additional statements for context.
3. **Perjury Exception:** Statements made under oath during plea proceedings may be used in perjury prosecutions.
4. **Third Party Use:** Statements may be admissible in proceedings against other defendants.

RULE 411. LIABILITY INSURANCE

Evidence that a person was or was not insured against liability is not admissible to prove whether the person acted negligently or otherwise wrongfully. But the court may admit this evidence for another purpose, such as proving a witness's bias or prejudice or proving agency, ownership, or control.

Insurance Evidence

Policy Rationale:

- Prevent unfair prejudice (jury might find liability because defendant can afford judgment)
- Avoid irrelevant distraction from actual conduct

Prohibited Use: Cannot prove negligence or wrongful conduct.

Common Permitted Uses:

- Bias: Insurance company employee as witness
- Agency: Insurance investigator's authority
- Ownership: Insurance policy shows who owned property
- Control: Policy terms show who controlled premises

Strategic Considerations:

- Careful witness preparation to avoid mentioning insurance
- Immediate limiting instructions if insurance mentioned
- Consider mistrial motions for prejudicial disclosures

RULE 412. SEX-OFFENSE CASES; THE VICTIM'S SEXUAL BEHAVIOR OR PREDISPOSITION

A. Prohibited Uses

The following evidence is not admissible in a civil or criminal proceeding involving alleged sexual misconduct:

(1) evidence offered to prove that a victim engaged in other sexual behavior; or

(2) evidence offered to prove a victim's sexual predisposition.

B. Exceptions

(1) Criminal Cases: The court may admit the following evidence if it is otherwise admissible under these rules and its probative value substantially outweighs the danger of harm to any victim and of unfair prejudice to any party:

(A) evidence of specific instances of a victim's sexual behavior, if offered to prove that someone other than the defendant was the source of semen, injury, or other physical evidence;

(B) evidence of specific instances of a victim's sexual behavior with respect to the person accused of the sexual misconduct, if offered by the defendant to prove consent or if offered by the prosecutor; and

(C) evidence whose exclusion would violate the defendant's constitutional rights.

(2) Civil Cases: In a civil case, the court may admit evidence offered to prove a victim's sexual behavior or sexual predisposition if its probative value substantially outweighs the danger of harm to any victim and of unfair prejudice to any party. The court may admit evidence of a victim's reputation only if the victim has placed it in controversy.

C. Procedure

Before admitting evidence under this rule, the court must conduct an in camera hearing and give the victim and parties a right to attend and be heard. Any motion requesting admission of evidence under this rule must be filed under seal and served on all parties and the victim or the victim's representative.

The Rape Shield Rule

Policy Goals:

- Protect victims from harassment and humiliation
- Prevent irrelevant character assassination
- Encourage reporting of sexual offenses
- Focus trial on alleged incident, not victim's history

General Prohibition: Evidence of victim's other sexual behavior or sexual predisposition is inadmissible.

Criminal Case Exceptions (Rule 412(b)(1))

Exception A - Alternative Source:

- Specific instances only (not reputation/opinion)
- Must explain physical evidence (semen, injury, etc.)
- Must prove someone other than defendant was source

Exception B - Prior Acts with Defendant:

- Sexual behavior between victim and defendant
- Defendant may offer to prove consent
- Prosecutor may offer (e.g., to show pattern)

Exception C - Constitutional Rights:

- Due process and confrontation clause protections

- Rarely applied - must be compelling constitutional need

Civil Case Standards (Rule 412(b)(2))

1. Higher Standard: Probative value must "substantially outweigh" harm and prejudice.
2. Reputation Evidence: Only if victim placed reputation in controversy.
3. Broader Discretion: Courts have more flexibility than in criminal cases.

Procedural Requirements

1. In Camera Hearing: Required before admission of any Rule 412 evidence.
2. Sealed Motion: All requests must be filed under seal.
3. Notice to Victim: Victim has right to attend and be heard.
4. Specific Findings: Court must make detailed record of decision.

Strategic Considerations

For Defense:

- Carefully analyze constitutional necessity
- Focus on specific exceptions, not general character
- Prepare detailed offers of proof

- Consider alternative theories that don't require sexual history

For Prosecution:

- Object to fishing expeditions
- Emphasize privacy and harassment concerns
- Argue insufficient probative value
- Prepare victim for potential hearing

RULE 413. SIMILAR CRIMES IN SEXUAL-ASSAULT CASES

A. Permitted Uses. In a criminal case in which a defendant is accused of a sexual assault, the court may admit evidence that the defendant committed any other sexual assault. The evidence may be considered on any matter to which it is relevant.
B. Disclosure to the Defendant. If the prosecutor intends to offer this evidence, the prosecutor must disclose it to the defendant, including witnesses' statements or a summary of the expected testimony. The prosecutor must do so at least 15 days before trial or at a later time that the court may allow for good cause.
C. Effect on Other Rules. This rule does not limit the admission or consideration of evidence under any other rule.
D. Definition of "Sexual Assault." [Detailed definition including various federal sexual offenses]

RULE 414. SIMILAR CRIMES IN CHILD-MOLESTATION CASES

[Similar structure to Rule 413 but for child molestation offenses]

RULE 415. SIMILAR ACTS IN CIVIL CASES INVOLVING SEXUAL ASSAULT OR CHILD MOLESTATION

[Similar structure but applies to civil cases with modified standards]

The Propensity Exception

Controversial Rules: These rules create specific exception to Rule 404's character evidence prohibition for sexual offenses.

Policy Rationale:

- Recognition that sexual offenses often follow patterns
- Difficulty of proof in sexual assault cases
- Legislative determination that probative value justifies admission

Scope of Admission:

- "Any matter to which it is relevant" - very broad
- Can be used to prove propensity (unlike Rule 404(b))
- Subject to Rule 403 balancing

Key Procedural Requirements

1. Notice: 15-day pretrial notice requirement (similar to Rule 404(b)).
2. Rule 403 Still Applies: Courts must still balance probative value against prejudice.
3. Broad Relevance: Evidence admissible for any relevant purpose, including propensity.

Strategic and Ethical Considerations

Heightened Scrutiny: Many courts apply rigorous Rule 403 analysis given the prejudicial nature of sexual offense evidence.

Defense Strategy:

- Challenge similarity between acts
- Argue temporal remoteness
- Emphasize prejudicial impact
- Request detailed limiting instructions

Prosecution Strategy:

- Establish clear patterns of behavior
- Show distinctive methods or circumstances
- Provide timely notice and detailed proffer
- Address Rule 403 concerns proactively

Differences Between Criminal and Civil Applications

Criminal Cases (Rules 413-414):

- Broadly admissible "on any matter to which it is relevant"
- 15-day notice requirement
- Subject to Rule 403 balancing

Civil Cases (Rule 415):

- Same broad admissibility standard
- Modified procedural requirements
- Often lower stakes may affect Rule 403 analysis

ARTICLE IV SUMMARY AND EXAM STRATEGY

Most Frequently Tested Rules

1. Rule 401-403: Foundation of relevance analysis - appears on virtually every evidence exam.
2. Rule 404: Character evidence and prior bad acts - heavily tested in both criminal and civil contexts.
3. Rules 407-411: Policy exclusions - common in multiple choice and essay questions.
4. Rule 412: Rape shield rule - increasingly important and frequently tested.

Key Analytical Frameworks

Relevance Analysis (Rules 401-403):

1. Is evidence logically relevant? (Rule 401)

2. Is evidence legally relevant? (Rule 401)

3. Should relevant evidence be excluded? (Rule 403)

4. Consider alternatives and limiting instructions

Character Evidence Analysis (Rule 404):

1. Is this character evidence or specific act evidence?

2. If character evidence, what is the purpose?

3. Does an exception apply?

4. What method of proof is appropriate? (Rule 405)

5. Consider Rule 403 balancing

Prior Bad Acts Analysis (Rule 404(b)):

1. What is the specific non-character purpose?

2. Is the purpose material to the case?

3. Is there sufficient similarity/connection?

4. Does probative value survive Rule 403 balancing?

5. Are notice requirements satisfied?

Common Exam Fact Patterns

Character Evidence Scenarios:

- Criminal defendant offering evidence of good character
- Prosecutor responding with rebuttal evidence

- Self-defense cases involving victim's character
- Prior conviction impeachment of witnesses

Prior Bad Acts Scenarios:

- Similar fraud schemes (showing intent/plan)
- Prior violence (showing motive/identity)
- Domestic violence patterns (showing intent)
- Drug dealing experience (showing knowledge)

Policy Exclusion Scenarios:

- Post-accident repairs and safety measures
- Settlement negotiations and offers
- Insurance coverage references
- Medical expense payments

Sexual Assault Evidence:

- Rape shield rule applications
- Prior sexual assault evidence
- Constitutional confrontation issues

Strategic Study Tips

For Multiple Choice:

- Memorize the specific exceptions and requirements
- Focus on distinguishing similar concepts (habit vs. character, character vs. specific acts)
- Understand procedural requirements (notice, hearings, jury instructions)

For Essays:

- Use systematic analytical frameworks
- Address Rule 403 balancing explicitly
- Consider alternative purposes for evidence
- Discuss procedural requirements and strategic considerations

Common Mistakes to Avoid:

- Confusing relevance with admissibility
- Setting relevance standard too high (remember "any tendency")
- Failing to identify specific Rule 404(b) purposes
- Forgetting Rule 403 balancing analysis
- Mixing up civil and criminal character evidence rules

Practical Application Tips

For Practitioners:

- Master the foundational relevance analysis
- Understand strategic implications of character evidence
- Know procedural requirements for prior bad acts
- Prepare for Rule 403 balancing arguments
- Consider ethical implications of sensitive evidence

Pretrial Practice:

- File motions in limine on character evidence issues
- Provide proper notice for Rule 404(b) evidence
- Seek pretrial rulings on policy exclusions
- Prepare detailed offers of proof

- Consider stipulations to avoid prejudicial evidence

Trial Practice:

- Make specific objections with clear grounds
- Request limiting instructions when appropriate
- Prepare witnesses to avoid improper character references
- Use Rule 106 to complete partial presentations
- Be ready with Rule 403 arguments

Relationship to Other Articles

1. Article VI (Witnesses): Character evidence for truthfulness (Rules 607-609) works with Rule 404(a)(3).
2. Article VIII (Hearsay): Prior statements may implicate both hearsay and character evidence rules.
3. Article VII (Expert Testimony): Expert opinions about character or behavioral patterns must satisfy both relevance and expert testimony requirements.

Constitutional Law: Due process and confrontation clause issues frequently arise with character evidence, especially in criminal cases.

Final Reminders

1. Rule 401-403 Foundation: Every piece of evidence must pass relevance analysis before considering other rules.
2. Rule 404 Prohibition: Character evidence to prove conduct is generally prohibited - look for specific exceptions.
3. Rule 403 Balancing: Always consider whether probative value is substantially outweighed by prejudicial dangers.
4. Procedural Requirements: Notice, hearings, and jury instructions are often required for sensitive evidence.
5. Policy Considerations: Understand the social policies underlying each rule to apply them appropriately in borderline cases.

Article IV represents the core of evidence law. Master these concepts and you'll have a solid foundation for understanding how evidence works in practice. The relevance framework established here applies throughout all other evidence rules, making this article essential for both exam success and effective legal practice.

Article V – Privileges

Rule 501 preserves testimonial privileges by deferring to federal common law in federal question cases and state law in diversity cases. Privileges protect confidential communications in relationships society values, including attorney-client, spousal communications, and psychotherapist-patient relationships. These protections encourage candid communications despite excluding relevant evidence.

RULE 501. PRIVILEGE IN GENERAL

The common law—as interpreted by United States courts in the light of reason and experience—governs a claim of privilege unless any of the following provides otherwise:

- the United States Constitution;
- a federal statute; or
- rules prescribed by the Supreme Court.

But in a civil case, state law governs privilege regarding a claim or defense for which state law supplies the rule of decision.

Understanding Privileges

Core Concept: A privilege allows a person to refuse to disclose information or to prevent others from disclosing it, even when the information is relevant and material to the case.

Policy Rationale

Privileges sacrifice truth-seeking to protect important relationships and interests:

- Encourage open communication in vital relationships
- Protect individual privacy and autonomy
- Support institutional functions (government, religion)
- Promote professional effectiveness (legal advice, medical treatment)

Federal vs. State Law (Erie Doctrine Application)

Federal Question Cases:

- Federal common law governs privileges
- Courts develop privilege law case-by-case
- Must consider "reason and experience"

Diversity Cases:

- State privilege law applies
- Follows substantive law of the forum state
- Can create complex choice-of-law issues

Mixed Cases:

- Federal claims: federal privilege law

- State claims: state privilege law
- Courts may need to apply different rules to different claims

Major Federal Privileges

Attorney-Client Privilege

Elements:

1. Communication between attorney and client

2. Made in confidence (no third parties present)

3. For purpose of seeking/providing legal advice

4. Privilege not waived

Scope:

- Covers communications, not underlying facts
- Extends to agents (paralegals, investigators)
- Applies to prospective clients
- Survives client's death

Common Issues:

- Corporate clients: Privilege limited to employees authorized to seek legal advice
- Joint representation: Privilege doesn't apply between co-clients
- Crime-fraud exception: No privilege for communications in furtherance of future crimes

Waiver:

- Voluntary disclosure to third parties
- Subject matter waiver for related communications
- Inadvertent disclosure may or may not waive (depends on circumstances)

Work Product Doctrine

Not technically a privilege but provides similar protection for attorney mental processes.

Two Types:

- Ordinary work product: Discoverable if substantial need shown
- Opinion work product: Nearly absolute protection for mental impressions

Covers: Attorney notes, research, trial preparation materials, witness interview notes

Spousal Privileges

Two Distinct Privileges:

1. Spousal Testimony Privilege (Criminal Cases Only)

- Spouse of defendant may refuse to testify against defendant
- Belongs to testifying spouse, not defendant
- Only applies to valid marriages at time of trial

- Doesn't cover communications

2. Marital Communications Privilege

- Protects confidential communications during marriage
- Applies in civil and criminal cases
- Survives divorce and death
- Both spouses hold the privilege

Exceptions:

- Cases between spouses
- Child abuse cases
- Crimes against family members

Physician-Patient Privilege

Not recognized under federal common law in most circuits.

Where recognized:

- Limited to treatment relationship
- Doesn't apply to court-ordered examinations
- Patient holds the privilege
- Numerous exceptions (will contests, malpractice, etc.)

Psychotherapist-Patient Privilege

Recognized by Supreme Court in Jaffee v. Redmond (1996).

Scope:

- Licensed psychotherapists and social workers

- Communications made for diagnosis/treatment
- Patient holds privilege
- Extends to treatment notes and records

Strong Protection: Few exceptions recognized

Executive Privilege

Presidential communications with close advisors on official matters.

Limited Scope:

- Presumptive privilege only
- Must be overcome by showing specific need
- Doesn't apply to criminal proceedings involving president
- Strongest for military/diplomatic secrets

Other Potential Privileges

Clergy-Penitent: Widely recognized but scope varies

Journalist Shield: Some federal circuits recognize limited privilege

Accountant-Client: Generally not recognized in federal court

Parent-Child: Limited recognition in some contexts

Privilege Analysis Framework

Step 1: Identify Applicable Law

- Federal question or diversity case?
- Which privilege law applies?
- Any constitutional or statutory overrides?

Step 2: Establish Privilege Elements

- Does communication fit privilege requirements?
- Was confidentiality maintained?
- Who holds the privilege?

Step 3: Check for Exceptions

- Crime-fraud exception applicable?
- Subject matter exceptions?
- Statutory overrides?

Step 4: Consider Waiver

- Voluntary disclosure to third parties?
- Subject matter waiver?
- Inadvertent disclosure circumstances?

Step 5: Apply Balancing Test (if applicable)

- Some privileges require balancing
- Consider competing interests
- Least restrictive alternative analysis

Common Privilege Issues

Waiver Problems

Inadvertent Disclosure:

- Courts consider: reasonableness of precautions, promptness of rectification efforts, scope of disclosure
- May result in limited or no waiver if proper procedures followed

Subject Matter Waiver:

- Disclosure of part of privileged communication may waive privilege for entire subject
- Strategic consideration in document production

Selective Waiver:

- Generally not permitted - can't waive privilege for some purposes but not others
- Exception: some courts allow waiver to government but not to private parties

Corporate Privilege Issues

Upjohn Doctrine: Privilege applies to communications with any corporate employee if:

- Communication relates to employee's duties
- Employee knows communication is for legal advice
- Communication made at management's direction

Common Interest Doctrine: Jointly represented parties can share privileged information without waiving privilege

Crime-Fraud Exception

Requirements:

- Prima facie showing of crime or fraud
- Communication was in furtherance of the crime/fraud
- Client knew or should have known of illegal purpose

Standard: Preponderance of evidence in most circuits

Strategic Considerations

For Practitioners

1. Privilege Logs: Detailed descriptions required when withholding documents on privilege grounds
2. Privilege Review: Systematic review of documents before production to identify privileged materials
3. Common Interest Agreements: Written agreements to protect shared privileged information
4. Inadvertent Disclosure Protocols: Agreements on handling accidental disclosure of privileged materials

Litigation Strategy

Asserting Privileges:

- Raise at earliest opportunity
- Provide sufficient detail without waiving privilege
- Consider in camera review for close cases

Challenging Privileges:

- Attack privilege elements systematically
- Look for waiver through disclosure or conduct
- Consider crime-fraud exception arguments

Ethical Considerations

1. Client Counseling: Explain scope and limitations of privileges
2. Document Retention: Consider privilege implications of document destruction policies
3. Third Party Communications: Be careful about destroying privilege through unnecessary third party involvement

Exam Tips

Issue Spotting

- Look for confidential communications in professional relationships
- Consider federal vs. state law application
- Watch for waiver through disclosure or conduct
- Identify potential exceptions (crime-fraud, etc.)

Analysis Structure

1. Identify which privilege potentially applies

2. Determine governing law (federal vs. state)
3. Analyze privilege elements systematically
4. Consider exceptions and waivers
5. Apply balancing test if applicable

Common Testing Areas

- Attorney-client privilege scope and waiver
- Spousal privileges in criminal cases
- Federal vs. state privilege law application
- Crime-fraud exception requirements
- Work product doctrine distinctions

Practice Tips

- Master the basic elements of major privileges
- Understand waiver doctrines thoroughly
- Know when state vs. federal law applies
- Practice systematic privilege analysis
- Consider practical implications for case strategy

Key Takeaway: Privileges represent a balance between truth-seeking and protecting important relationships. Understanding their scope, exceptions, and waiver rules is essential for effective legal practice and exam success.

Article VI – Witnesses

This comprehensive article governs witness competency, examination procedures, and credibility determinations. It establishes requirements for personal knowledge and truthful testimony while providing methods for impeaching witness credibility. Rules 608-609, covering character for truthfulness and criminal conviction impeachment, are among the most frequently tested provisions in evidence law.

This article covers witness competency, credibility, and impeachment - fundamental concepts tested on every evidence exam.

RULE 601. COMPETENCY TO TESTIFY GENERALLY

Every person is competent to be a witness unless these rules provide otherwise. But in a civil case, state law governs the witness's competency regarding a claim or defense for which state law supplies the rule of decision.

Key Principle: Presumption of competency - everyone can testify unless specifically disqualified.

Federal vs. State Law: Same Erie doctrine application as privileges - state law governs competency in diversity cases.

RULE 602. NEED FOR PERSONAL KNOWLEDGE

A witness may testify to a matter only if evidence is introduced sufficient to support a finding that the witness has personal knowledge of the matter. Evidence to prove personal knowledge may consist of the witness's own testimony. This rule does not apply to a witness's expert testimony under Rule 702.

Foundation Requirement: Must establish witness observed, heard, or otherwise perceived the facts firsthand.

Standard: "Sufficient to support a finding" - low threshold, judge makes preliminary determination under Rule 104(b).

Examples:

- "I saw the accident happen"
- "I heard him say..."
- "I was present when..."

Not Personal Knowledge:

- Speculation or guesswork
- Information from others (hearsay)
- Conclusions without factual basis

RULE 603. OATH OR AFFIRMATION TO TESTIFY TRUTHFULLY

Before testifying, a witness must give an oath or affirmation to testify truthfully. It must be in a form designed to impress the witness with the duty to testify truthfully.

Flexibility: Accommodates religious beliefs and personal preferences - oath or affirmation acceptable.

RULE 604. INTERPRETER

An interpreter must be qualified and must give an oath or affirmation to make a true translation.

RULE 605. JUDGE'S COMPETENCY AS A WITNESS

The presiding judge may not testify as a witness at the trial. A party need not object to preserve the issue.

Absolute Prohibition: No exceptions, automatic reversible error.

RULE 606. JUROR'S COMPETENCY AS A WITNESS

A. At the Trial. A juror may not testify as a witness before the other jurors at the trial. If a juror is called to testify, the court must give the opposing party an opportunity to object outside the jury's presence.
B. During an Inquiry into the Validity of a Verdict or Indictment.

(1) Prohibited testimony. During an inquiry into the validity of a verdict or indictment, a juror may not testify about any statement made or incident that occurred during the jury's deliberations; the effect of anything on that juror's or another juror's vote; or that juror's mental processes concerning the

verdict or indictment. The court may not receive a juror's affidavit or evidence of a juror's statement on these matters.

(2) Exceptions. A juror may testify about whether:

(a) extraneous prejudicial information was improperly brought to the jury's attention;

(b) an outside influence was improperly brought to bear on any juror; or

(c) a mistake was made in entering the verdict on the verdict form.

Internal vs. External Influences:

- Internal (inadmissible): Juror opinions, arguments, mental processes, misunderstanding of law
- External (admissible): Outside research, contact with parties, bribery attempts, clerical errors

RULE 607. WHO MAY IMPEACH A WITNESS

Any party, including the party that called the witness, may attack the witness's credibility.

1. Abolishes Voucher Rule: Calling party no longer "vouches" for witness's credibility and can impeach if witness gives unexpected testimony.
2. Strategic Use: Allows preemptive impeachment of required witnesses.

RULE 608. A WITNESS'S CHARACTER FOR TRUTHFULNESS OR UNTRUTHFULNESS

A. Reputation or Opinion Evidence. A witness's credibility may be attacked or supported by testimony about the witness's reputation for having a character for truthfulness or untruthfulness, or by testimony in the form of an opinion about that character. But evidence of truthful character is admissible only after the witness's character for truthfulness has been attacked.
B. Specific Instances of Conduct. Except for a criminal conviction under Rule 609, extrinsic evidence is not admissible to prove specific instances of the witness's conduct in order to attack or support the witness's character for truthfulness. But the court may, on cross-examination, allow them to be asked about if they are probative of the character for truthfulness or untruthfulness.

Character for Truthfulness - Rule 608(a)

Methods of Proof: Reputation and opinion only (same as Rule 405).

Rehabilitation Timing: Can only offer evidence of truthful character AFTER credibility has been attacked.

Foundation Requirements:

- Witness must know the person's reputation in relevant community

- Opinion must be based on adequate personal knowledge
- Must specify truthfulness/untruthfulness trait

Specific Instances of Conduct - Rule 608(b)

"Extrinsic Evidence" Prohibition: Cannot prove specific bad acts through documents, other witnesses, or physical evidence.

Cross-Examination Allowed: May ask about specific acts if:

- Probative of truthfulness/untruthfulness
- Good faith basis for question
- Must "take the answer" - cannot contradict with other evidence

Examples of Probative Acts:

- Perjury, fraud, filing false documents
- Acts involving dishonesty or false statement
- NOT: violence, drug use, adultery (unless involving deception)

Strategic Considerations:

- Risk of opening door to rehabilitation
- Witness may deny and you cannot prove it
- May backfire if witness explains convincingly

RULE 609. IMPEACHMENT BY EVIDENCE OF A CRIMINAL CONVICTION

A. In General. The following rules apply to attacking a witness's character for truthfulness by evidence of a criminal conviction:

(1) for a crime that, in the convicting jurisdiction, was punishable by death or by imprisonment for more than one year, the evidence:

(a) must be admitted, subject to Rule 403, in a civil case or in a criminal case in which the witness is not a defendant; or

(b) must be admitted in a criminal case in which the witness is a defendant, if the probative value of the evidence outweighs its prejudicial effect to that defendant; and

(2) for any crime regardless of the punishment, if the court can readily determine that establishing the elements of the crime required proving or the witness's admitting a dishonest act or false statement.

B. Limit on Using the Evidence After 10 Years. This subdivision (b) applies if more than 10 years have passed since the witness's conviction or release from confinement for it, whichever is later. Evidence of the conviction is admissible only if:

(a) its probative value, supported by specific facts and circumstances, substantially outweighs its prejudicial effect; and

(b) the proponent gives an adverse party reasonable written notice of the intent to use it so that the party has a fair opportunity to contest its use.

Prior Conviction Impeachment Framework

Two Categories of Convictions:

Category 1: Felonies (Rule 609(a)(1))

- Punishable by death or imprisonment > 1 year
- Applies regardless of actual sentence imposed
- Different standards for different witnesses

Category 2: Dishonesty Crimes (Rule 609(a)(2))

- Any crime requiring proof of dishonest act or false statement
- Automatic admission regardless of punishment level
- Examples: perjury, fraud, theft, forgery

Balancing Standards

1. Civil Cases & Criminal Non-Defendant Witnesses: Regular Rule 403 balancing (probative value substantially outweighed by prejudice).
2. Criminal Defendant Witnesses: Reverse Rule 403 (probative value must outweigh prejudicial effect to defendant) - higher bar for admission.
3. Dishonesty Crimes: No balancing - automatically admissible.

Ten-Year Rule (Rule 609(b))

1. When Applicable: More than 10 years since conviction OR release from confinement, whichever is later.
2. Standard: Probative value must "substantially outweigh" prejudicial effect - very high bar.
3. Notice Requirement: Written notice required for remote convictions.

Impeachment Strategy

For Cross-Examiner:

- Research witness's criminal history thoroughly
- Prepare specific questions about convictions
- Consider strategic value vs. potential sympathy for witness
- Have certified records available

For Direct Examiner:

- Consider bringing out convictions on direct examination
- Prepare witness for cross-examination
- Emphasize rehabilitation and changed circumstances
- Object to improper questions about arrests or dismissed charges

RULE 610. RELIGIOUS BELIEFS OR OPINIONS

Evidence of a witness's religious beliefs or opinions is not admissible to attack or support the witness's credibility.

Absolute Prohibition: Cannot use religious beliefs to impeach or support credibility.

Exception: Religious beliefs may be relevant to bias (e.g., shared religious affiliation with party).

RULE 611. MODE AND ORDER OF EXAMINING WITNESSES AND PRESENTING EVIDENCE

A. Control by the Court; Purposes. The court should exercise reasonable control over the mode and order of examining witnesses and presenting evidence so as to:

(1) make those procedures effective for determining the truth;

(2) avoid wasting time; and

(3) protect witnesses from harassment or undue embarrassment.

B. Scope of Cross-Examination. Cross-examination should not go beyond the subject matter of the direct examination and matters affecting the witness's credibility. The court may allow inquiry into additional matters as if on direct examination.

C. Leading Questions. Leading questions should not be used on direct examination except as necessary to develop the witness's testimony. Ordinarily, the court should allow leading questions:

(1) on cross-examination;

(2) when a party calls a hostile witness, an adverse party, or a witness identified with an adverse party.

Scope of Cross-Examination

1. General Rule: Limited to subjects covered on direct examination plus credibility.
2. "Door Opening": Direct examination determines what subjects are fair game for cross.
3. Court Discretion: Judge may allow broader cross-examination with questioning treated as direct.

Leading Questions

Direct Examination: Generally prohibited except:

- Hostile witnesses
- Adverse parties
- Background/preliminary matters
- Refreshing recollection
- Child or impaired witnesses

Cross-Examination: Presumptively allowed.

RULE 612. WRITING USED TO REFRESH A WITNESS'S MEMORY

A. Scope. This rule gives an adverse party certain options when a witness uses a writing to refresh memory:

(1) while testifying; or

(2) before testifying, if the court decides that justice requires the party to have those options.

B. Adverse Party's Options. Unless the court orders otherwise under Rule 26(c), an adverse party is entitled to have the writing produced at the hearing, to inspect it, to cross-examine the witness about it, and to introduce in evidence any portion that relates to the witness's testimony.

Present Recollection Refreshed

Process:

1. Witness testifies to lack of present memory

2. Document shown to witness to refresh memory

3. Document removed

4. Witness testifies from refreshed memory

5. Opponent entitled to examine refreshing document

Key Points:

- Witness must testify from memory, not from document
- Any writing can be used to refresh (even inadmissible documents)
- Opponent can cross-examine about and introduce relevant portions

Distinguished from Past Recollection Recorded: Here witness remembers after refreshing; in past recollection recorded, witness still cannot remember.

RULE 613. WITNESS'S PRIOR STATEMENT

A. Showing or Disclosing the Statement During Examination. When examining a witness about the witness's prior statement, a party need not show it or disclose its contents to the witness. But the party must, on request, show it or disclose its contents to an adverse party's attorney.

B. Extrinsic Evidence of a Prior Inconsistent Statement. Extrinsic evidence of a witness's prior inconsistent statement is admissible only if the witness is given an opportunity to explain or deny the statement and an adverse party is given an opportunity to examine the witness about it, or if justice so requires. This subdivision (b) does not apply to an opposing party's statement under Rule 801(d)(2).

Prior Inconsistent Statements

Foundation Requirements (Rule 613(b)):

- Witness must have opportunity to explain or deny
- Opponent must have opportunity to examine about statement
- Order flexible - can confront witness after extrinsic evidence

Exceptions:

- Party admissions (Rule 801(d)(2)) - no foundation required
- Justice requires different treatment

Strategic Use:

- Powerful impeachment tool
- Must have good faith basis
- Consider whether statement is admissible for truth (Rule 801(d)(1))

RULE 614. COURT'S CALLING OR EXAMINING A WITNESS

The court may call its own witnesses or examine any witness.

Rare in Practice: Judges seldom call witnesses but may examine for clarification.

RULE 615. EXCLUDING WITNESSES

At a party's request, the court must order witnesses excluded so that they cannot hear other witnesses' testimony. Or the court may do so on its own. But this rule does not authorize excluding:

(a) a party who is a natural person;

(b) an officer or employee of a party that is not a natural person, after being designated as the party's representative by its attorney;

(c) a person whose presence a party shows to be essential to presenting the party's case; or

(d) a person authorized by statute to be present.

Witness Sequestration

Purpose: Prevent witnesses from conforming testimony to what others have said.

Mandatory: Court must exclude witnesses when requested by any party.

Exceptions:

- Natural person parties
- Corporate representatives (one per party)
- Essential persons (experts, investigating officers)
- Statutorily authorized persons (victim advocates)

Practical Effects:

- Witnesses wait outside courtroom
- Cannot discuss testimony with other witnesses
- May affect witness preparation strategies

ARTICLE VI SUMMARY AND STRATEGY

Key Testing Areas

Impeachment Methods:

- Character for truthfulness (Rule 608)
- Prior convictions (Rule 609)
- Prior inconsistent statements (Rule 613)
- Bias evidence

Examination Rules:

- Scope of cross-examination

- Leading questions
- Present recollection refreshed

Competency Issues:

- Personal knowledge requirement
- Judge and juror testimony prohibition

Common Exam Scenarios

Prior Conviction Impeachment:

- Determining admissibility under Rule 609
- Balancing tests for different types of witnesses
- Ten-year rule applications

Character for Truthfulness:

- When reputation/opinion evidence is admissible
- Specific instances on cross-examination
- Extrinsic evidence prohibition

Witness Examination:

- Proper scope of cross-examination
- Leading question rules
- Document refreshing procedures

Strategic Considerations

Impeachment Decisions:

- Cost-benefit analysis of attacking credibility

- Risk of rehabilitation
- Jury sympathy considerations

Examination Strategy:

- Order of witnesses and evidence
- Use of leading questions
- Document preparation and refreshing

Credibility Enhancement:

- Timing of rehabilitation
- Methods of supporting truthfulness
- Addressing impeachment proactively

Practice Tips

- Master the different impeachment methods and their requirements
- Understand balancing standards for prior conviction evidence
- Know the exceptions to general examination rules
- Practice systematic credibility analysis
- Consider ethical implications of impeachment strategies

Key Takeaway: Article VI provides the framework for presenting and challenging witness testimony. Understanding these rules is essential for effective trial advocacy and evidence analysis.

Article VII – Opinions and Expert Testimony

These rules distinguish between permissible lay opinions under Rule 701 and expert testimony governed by Rules 702-706. Expert witnesses must possess adequate qualifications, employ reliable methodologies, and provide testimony that assists the trier of fact. The Daubert reliability standard has made expert testimony admissibility decisions increasingly sophisticated and consequential.

This article governs when witnesses may offer opinion testimony and establishes the framework for expert testimony reliability.

RULE 701. OPINION TESTIMONY BY LAY WITNESSES

If a witness is not testifying as an expert, testimony in the form of an opinion is limited to one that is:

(a) rationally based on the witness's perception;

(b) helpful to clearly understanding the witness's testimony or to determining a fact in issue; and

(c) not based on scientific, technical, or other specialized knowledge within the scope of Rule 702.

Lay Opinion Requirements

Three-Part Test:

1. Rationally Based on Perception

- Must be based on firsthand observation
- Cannot be speculation or conjecture
- Must flow logically from what witness observed

2. Helpful to Understanding

- Assists jury in understanding facts
- More efficient than describing all underlying observations
- Shorthand for complex sensory impressions

3. Not Expert Knowledge

- Cannot require specialized training or education
- Must be within common experience
- Bright line between lay and expert testimony

Permissible Lay Opinions

Classic Examples:

- Speed of vehicle: "The car was going very fast"
- Intoxication: "He appeared drunk"
- Emotional state: "She seemed angry"
- Physical appearance: "He looked tired"
- Voice identification: "That sounded like John"
- Handwriting recognition: "That's Mary's writing"

Recent Expansions:

- Drug use based on observation of behavior
- Value of property (if owner or familiar with area)
- Business practices (if experienced in the field)

Impermissible Lay Opinions

Requires Expert Knowledge:

- Medical diagnoses
- Legal conclusions
- Technical causation
- Complex valuations
- Scientific determinations

Ultimate Issue Problems:

- "The defendant was negligent" (legal conclusion)
- "The contract was breached" (legal standard application)
- "The injuries were caused by the accident" (complex causation)

Strategic Considerations

For Proponents:

- Lay opinion often more persuasive than expert testimony
- Less expensive than hiring experts
- Can be more relatable to jury

For Opponents:

- Challenge the perception foundation
- Argue opinion requires expert knowledge
- Object to legal conclusions

RULE 702. TESTIMONY BY EXPERT WITNESSES

A witness who is qualified as an expert by knowledge, skill, experience, training, or education may testify in the form of an opinion or otherwise if:

(a) the expert's scientific, technical, or other specialized knowledge will help the trier of fact to understand the evidence or to determine a fact in issue;

(b) the testimony is based on sufficient facts or data;

(c) the testimony is the product of reliable principles and methods; and

(d) the expert has reliably applied the principles and methods to the facts of the case.

The Daubert Revolution

1. Pre-Daubert (Frye Test): Expert testimony admissible if based on methods "generally accepted" in relevant scientific community.
2. Daubert v. Merrell Dow (1993): Supreme Court held Rule 702 superseded Frye test, making judges "gatekeepers" for scientific reliability.

3. Post-Daubert Evolution: Extended beyond science to all expert testimony in Kumho Tire (1999).

Four-Part Daubert/Rule 702 Analysis

1. Qualification

- Knowledge, skill, experience, training, or education
- Must be relevant to subject matter
- Formal credentials not required
- Experience alone can qualify

2. Helpfulness

- Will assist trier of fact
- Subject beyond common knowledge
- Fits the facts of the case
- Not cumulative or confusing

3. Reliability

- Based on sufficient facts or data
- Product of reliable principles and methods
- Consider Daubert factors (when applicable)

4. Proper Application

- Expert reliably applied methods to case facts
- No analytical gap between data and conclusion
- Methods appropriate for this case

Daubert Reliability Factors

For Scientific Evidence:

- Testing: Has theory/technique been tested?
- Peer Review: Published in peer-reviewed journals?
- Error Rate: Known or potential rate of error?
- Standards: Existence of standards controlling operation?
- General Acceptance: Acceptance in relevant community?

Flexible Application: Factors are illustrative, not mandatory checklist.

Types of Expert Testimony

Scientific Experts:

- Medical professionals
- Engineers and scientists
- Forensic specialists
- Statistical analysts

Technical Experts:

- Accident reconstructionists
- Computer specialists
- Industry professionals
- Skilled tradespeople

Experience-Based Experts:

- Law enforcement officers

- Business valuators
- Art authenticators
- Agricultural specialists

Qualification Standards

Liberal Standard: Wide range of backgrounds can qualify as experts.

Examples:

- Physician qualified to testify about medical causation
- Police officer qualified to testify about drug transactions
- Mechanic qualified to testify about vehicle defects
- Accountant qualified to testify about business valuations

Degree of Qualification: Goes to weight, not admissibility.

Reliability Analysis

Judge as Gatekeeper: Rule 104(a) preliminary question - judge decides admissibility.

Preponderance Standard: Judge must find reliability by preponderance of evidence.

Flexible Inquiry: Consider totality of circumstances, not rigid checklist.

Common Reliability Issues:

- Inadequate data foundation

- Methodology not suited to case facts
- Lack of testing or validation
- Excessive speculation or conjecture

RULE 703. BASES OF AN EXPERT'S OPINION TESTIMONY

An expert may base an opinion on facts or data in the case that the expert has been made aware of or personally observed. If experts in the particular field would reasonably rely on those kinds of facts or data in forming an opinion on the subject, they need not be admissible in evidence in order for the opinion to be admitted. But if the facts or data would otherwise be inadmissible, the proponent must not disclose them to the jury unless the court determines that their probative value in helping the jury evaluate the expert's opinion substantially outweighs their prejudicial effect.

Three Types of Expert Opinion Bases

1. Personal Observation

- Expert personally observed facts
- Most reliable foundation
- No hearsay concerns

2. Admissible Evidence

- Facts or data already in evidence
- Hypothetical questions based on trial evidence
- Documents and exhibits admitted at trial

3. Inadmissible Evidence (Rule 703 Exception)

- Information experts in field reasonably rely on
- Medical records, police reports, industry studies
- Subject to balancing test for disclosure

THE RULE 703 BALANCING TEST

When Inadmissible Information Used:

- May form basis for expert opinion
- Generally cannot be disclosed to jury

Exception: probative value substantially outweighs prejudicial effect

Strategic Implications:

- Expert can rely on hearsay in forming opinion
- Cannot use expert as conduit for inadmissible evidence
- Careful foundation required for disclosure

RULE 704. OPINION ON AN ULTIMATE ISSUE

(a) In General. An opinion is not objectionable just because it embraces an ultimate issue.

(b) Exception. In a criminal case, an expert witness must not state an opinion about whether the defendant did or did not have a mental state or condition that constitutes an element of the crime or of a defense. Those matters are for the trier of fact alone.

Ultimate Issue Testimony

General Rule: Experts may testify on ultimate issues in the case.

Examples:

- "The accident was caused by brake failure"
- "The defendant was insane at the time"
- "The contract was breached"

Criminal Case Exception: Cannot testify that defendant had required mental state (intent, knowledge, etc.).

Rationale: Preserve jury's role in determining criminal culpability.

RULE 705. DISCLOSING THE FACTS OR DATA UNDERLYING AN EXPERT'S OPINION

Unless the court orders otherwise, an expert may state an opinion—and give the reasons for it—without first testifying to the underlying facts or data. But the expert may be required to disclose those facts or data on cross-examination.

Opinion-First Rule

Traditional Approach: Expert first testified to facts, then gave opinion.

Modern Approach: Expert may give opinion first, explain basis on cross-examination.

Strategic Advantages:

- More persuasive presentation
- Avoids boring jury with technical details
- Focuses on conclusions first

Cross-Examination Rights: Opponent can explore underlying facts and methodology.

RULE 706. COURT-APPOINTED EXPERT WITNESSES

(a) Appointment Process. On a party's motion or on its own, the court may order the parties to show cause why expert witnesses should not be appointed, and may ask the parties to submit nominations. The court may appoint any expert that the parties agree on and any of its own choosing. But the court may only appoint someone who consents to act.

(b) Expert's Role. The court must inform the expert of the expert's duties. The expert:

- must advise the parties of any findings the expert makes;
- may be deposed by any party;
- may be called to testify by the court or any party; and
- may be cross-examined by any party, including the party that called the expert.

(c) Compensation. The expert's reasonable compensation is paid by the parties in any proportion and manner that the court directs, and the compensation is taxable as costs.

Court-Appointed Experts

Rare in Practice: Judges seldom appoint their own experts.

When Used:

- Complex technical issues
- Battle of experts with conflicting conclusions
- Need for neutral perspective
- Court lacks confidence in party experts

Procedural Protections:

- Parties may cross-examine court's expert
- Expert's findings must be shared with all parties
- Compensation shared among parties

Expert Testimony Strategy and Practice

Daubert Hearings

1. Pre-Trial Reliability Challenges:

- Motion practice to exclude unreliable expert testimony
- Burden on proponent to show reliability
- Detailed examination of methodology and application

2. Hearing Procedures:

- Outside presence of jury
- Expert may testify about methodology
- Consider scientific literature and peer review
- Judge makes reliability determination

Common Daubert Challenges

1. Insufficient Data Foundation:

- Expert opinion based on too little information
- Failure to consider alternative explanations
- Inadequate investigation or testing

2. Methodology Problems:

- Novel or untested methods
- Inappropriate application of valid methods
- Lack of scientific rigor
- Excessive speculation

3. Qualifications Issues:

- Expert lacks relevant experience
- No background in specific area of testimony
- Insufficient education or training

Strategic Considerations

For Proponents:

- Thoroughly vet expert qualifications and methodology
- Prepare for Daubert challenges
- Consider alternative experts if reliability questionable
- Build strong foundation for opinions

For Opponents:

- Research expert's background and prior testimony
- Challenge methodology and application

- Highlight limitations and assumptions
- Consider own expert to rebut

Expert Witness Preparation

Qualification Phase:

- Education, training, experience
- Prior testimony and publications
- Professional associations and awards
- Relevant background for this case

Opinion Phase:

- Clear statement of conclusions
- Explanation of methodology
- Basis for opinions
- Limitations and assumptions

Cross-Examination Preparation:

- Anticipate attacks on methodology
- Prepare responses to hypotheticals
- Understand literature in the field
- Be ready to defend assumptions

Common Expert Testimony Issues

Bias and Advocacy:

- Financial interest in outcome
- Relationship with attorney or party

- Pattern of testifying for one side
- Advocacy vs. neutral expertise

Scope of Expertise:

- Testifying beyond qualifications
- Opinions on legal standards
- Speculation beyond data
- Failure to acknowledge limitations

Communication Issues:

- Complex jargon confusing to jury
- Failure to explain methodology clearly
- Inconsistent with prior positions
- Overstatement of conclusions

ARTICLE VII SUMMARY AND EXAM STRATEGY

Key Testing Areas

Lay vs. Expert Opinion:

- When lay witness can give opinion
- Requirements for expert qualification
- Boundary between lay and expert testimony

Daubert/Rule 702 Analysis:

- Four-part reliability test
- Judicial gatekeeping role
- Scientific vs. experience-based expertise

Expert Opinion Bases:

- Types of information experts can rely on
- Rule 703 balancing for inadmissible information
- Foundation requirements

Common Exam Scenarios

Expert Qualification:

- Whether witness has sufficient background
- Relevance of experience to testimony
- Formal vs. practical qualifications

Reliability Challenges:

- Novel scientific techniques
- Insufficient data foundation
- Inappropriate methodology
- Speculative conclusions

Opinion Scope:

- Ultimate issue testimony
- Mental state opinions in criminal cases
- Legal vs. factual conclusions

Strategic Study Tips

For Multiple Choice:

- Master the four-part Rule 702 test
- Understand lay opinion limitations

- Know the bases for expert opinions
- Remember criminal case mental state exception

For Essays:

- Use systematic Daubert analysis
- Consider both qualification and reliability
- Address Rule 703 foundation issues
- Discuss strategic implications

Practice Applications

Effective Expert Use:

- Select qualified experts with relevant experience
- Ensure reliable methodology and adequate foundation
- Prepare for Daubert challenges
- Focus on clear communication to jury

Expert Challenges:

- Research expert's background and prior testimony
- Challenge methodology, not just conclusions
- Highlight limitations and assumptions
- Consider timing of challenges (pre-trial vs. trial)

Key Takeaway: Article VII establishes the framework for opinion testimony, with expert testimony requiring careful attention to qualification, reliability, and proper foundation. Understanding these requirements is essential for effective use and challenge of expert evidence.

ARTICLE VIII – HEARSAY

Hearsay represents the most complex and extensively tested area of evidence law. The article defines hearsay, identifies exclusions from the definition, and establishes numerous exceptions based on circumstantial guarantees of reliability. Rules 803-804 contain over thirty exceptions, making systematic analysis essential for understanding when out-of-court statements may be admitted.

The most complex and heavily tested area of evidence law. Master the definition, exclusions, and exceptions for exam success.

RULE 801. DEFINITIONS THAT APPLY TO THIS ARTICLE; EXCLUSIONS FROM HEARSAY

A. Statement

"Statement" means a person's oral assertion, written assertion, or nonverbal conduct, if the person intended it as an assertion.

B. Declarant

"Declarant" means the person who made the statement.

C. Hearsay

"Hearsay" means a statement that:

(1) the declarant made while not testifying at the current trial or hearing; and

(2) a party offers in evidence to prove the truth of the matter asserted in the statement.

D. Statements That Are Not Hearsay

A statement that meets the following conditions is not hearsay:

(1) A Declarant-Witness's Prior Statement. The declarant testifies and is subject to cross-examination about a prior statement, and the statement:

(a) is inconsistent with the declarant's testimony and was given under penalty of perjury at a trial, hearing, or other proceeding or in a deposition; or

(b) is consistent with the declarant's testimony and is offered to rebut an express or implied charge that the declarant recently fabricated it or acted from a recent improper influence or motive in so testifying; or

(c) identifies a person as someone the declarant perceived earlier.

(2) An Opposing Party's Statement. The statement is offered against a party and:

(a) was made by the party in an individual or representative capacity;

(b) is one the party manifested that it adopted or believed to be true;

(c) was made by a person whom the party authorized to make a statement on the subject;

(d) was made by the party's agent or employee on a matter within the scope of that relationship and while it existed; or

(e) was made by the party's coconspirator during and in furtherance of the conspiracy.

Understanding Hearsay - The Foundation

The Basic Definition

Hearsay = Out-of-Court Statement + Offered for Truth

Three Elements:

1. Statement: Oral, written, or assertive conduct

2. Out-of-court: Made while not testifying at current proceeding

3. Offered for truth: Proponent seeks to prove the statement is accurate

The Hearsay Dangers

Why Exclude Hearsay:

- No oath: Declarant not under oath when statement made
- No demeanor: Jury cannot observe declarant's demeanor

- No cross-examination: Cannot test declarant's perception, memory, narration, sincerity

The Theory: These safeguards ensure reliability of testimony.

Step-by-Step Hearsay Analysis

Step 1: Is it a statement?

- Oral or written words
- Nonverbal conduct intended as assertion
- Not: questions, commands, non-assertive conduct

Step 2: Made out-of-court?

- While not testifying at current trial/hearing
- Includes prior testimony at different proceedings

Step 3: Offered to prove truth of matter asserted?

- What is the matter asserted in the statement?
- Why is the proponent offering the statement?
- If offered for truth = hearsay (unless exception applies)

Step 4: Does exclusion or exception apply?

- Rule 801(d) exclusions
- Rule 803 exceptions (declarant availability immaterial)
- Rule 804 exceptions (declarant unavailable)
- Rule 807 residual exception

Non-Hearsay Uses

Common Non-Truth Purposes:

Effect on Listener:

- Notice, knowledge, motive
- "He told me the bridge was out" (to show listener's knowledge)

Verbal Acts (Legally Operative Words):

- Contracts, gifts, defamation
- "I accept your offer" (creates legal relationship)

State of Mind of Speaker:

- Shows speaker's knowledge, intent, motive
- "I hate John" (shows speaker's feelings, not John's character)

Impeachment:

- Prior inconsistent statements (if not offered for truth)
- Shows witness said something different before

Context/Background:

- Explains subsequent conduct
- Provides narrative completeness

Assertive vs. Non-Assertive Conduct

Assertive Conduct (Can Be Hearsay):

- Pointing to identify someone

- Nodding head yes/no
- Sign language
- Must be intended as communication

Non-Assertive Conduct (Not Hearsay):

- Putting on coat (may show belief it's cold)
- Driving carefully (may show sobriety)
- Flight from scene (may show consciousness of guilt)

RULE 801(D) - EXCLUSIONS FROM HEARSAY

Prior Statements by Witness (Rule 801(d)(1))

Requirements for All Prior Statements:

- Declarant testifies at trial
- Subject to cross-examination about prior statement

Three Types:

1. (d)(1)(A) - Prior Inconsistent Statements

Requirements:

- Inconsistent with trial testimony
- Given under penalty of perjury
- At trial, hearing, proceeding, or deposition

Key Point: Must be under oath - excludes most police station statements.

Example: Witness testifies defendant was not at scene, but previously testified under oath at preliminary hearing that defendant was there.

2. (d)(1)(B) - Prior Consistent Statements

Requirements:

- Consistent with trial testimony
- Offered to rebut charge of recent fabrication or improper influence/motive
- Statement made before alleged fabrication or improper influence

Timing Critical: Statement must predate the claimed motive to fabricate.

Example: Witness claims defendant threatened her. If defense argues witness fabricated story after being promised reward, prosecution can offer witness's consistent statement made before reward was offered.

3. (d)(1)(C) - Prior Identification

Requirements:

- Statement identifies person
- Based on declarant's earlier perception
- Declarant testifies and subject to cross-examination

Broad Application: Includes lineups, photo arrays, voice identification.

Example: Witness identifies defendant at trial and previously identified defendant in lineup.

Opposing Party Statements (Rule 801(d)(2))

General Principle: Anything said by opposing party can be used against them - no hearsay problem.

1. (d)(2)(A) - Individual or Representative Statements

Individual Capacity: Party's own words.

Representative Capacity: Statements made on behalf of organization when authorized to speak.

2. (d)(2)(B) - Adoptive Admissions

Requirements:

- Party adopted or manifested belief in statement's truth
- Can be express or implied adoption

Common Example: Silence in face of accusation (when reasonable person would deny).

Limitations: Consider circumstances - would reasonable person respond? Was party able to respond?

3. (d)(2)(C) - Authorized Statements

Requirements:

- Person authorized to speak on the subject
- Authorization can be express or implied

Examples: Corporate spokesperson, attorney, agent with speaking authority.

4. (d)(2)(D) - Employee/Agent Statements

Requirements:

- Made by employee or agent
- Concerning matter within scope of relationship
- During existence of relationship

Scope Questions:

- Must relate to employment duties
- Personal matters generally excluded
- Consider job description and circumstances

Example: Truck driver's statement about accident during delivery route admissible against employer.

5. (d)(2)(E) - Co-Conspirator Statements

Requirements:

- Statement by party's co-conspirator
- Made during conspiracy
- In furtherance of conspiracy

Bootstrapping Rule: Cannot use co-conspirator's statement alone to prove conspiracy existed.

"In Furtherance" Requirement: Must advance conspiracy goals - idle chatter insufficient.

RULE 802. THE RULE AGAINST HEARSAY

Hearsay is not admissible unless any of the following provides otherwise:

- a federal statute;
- these rules; or
- other rules prescribed by the Supreme Court.

Simple Rule: Hearsay inadmissible unless specific exception applies.

Sources of Exceptions:

- Federal Rules of Evidence (Rules 803, 804, 807)
- Federal statutes
- Constitutional requirements
- Other Supreme Court rules

RULE 803. EXCEPTIONS TO THE RULE AGAINST HEARSAY—REGARDLESS OF WHETHER THE DECLARANT IS AVAILABLE AS A WITNESS

Rule 803 contains 23 numbered exceptions that apply whether the declarant is available or unavailable.

Rule 803(1) - Present Sense Impression

A statement describing or explaining an event or condition, made while or immediately after the declarant perceived it.

Requirements:

- Describes event or condition
- Made while perceiving OR immediately after
- Personal perception by declarant

Rationale: Spontaneity reduces likelihood of fabrication.

Time Requirement: "Immediately after" - minutes or seconds, not hours.

Examples:

- "That car is running the red light" (while observing)
- "I just saw an accident" (immediately after)

Rule 803(2) - Excited Utterance

A statement relating to a startling event or condition, made while the declarant was under the stress of excitement that it caused.

Requirements:

- Startling event occurred
- Statement relates to the event
- Made while under stress of excitement from event

Key Difference from Present Sense Impression:

- Longer time period allowed
- Focuses on continued excitement/stress
- Must be startling event (more than just observable)

Examples:

- "He shot me!" (said by victim in ambulance)
- "The brakes failed!" (said after car accident)

Rule 803(3) - Then-Existing Mental, Emotional, or Physical Condition

A statement of the declarant's then-existing state of mind (such as motive, intent, or plan) or emotional, physical, or mental condition (such as mental feeling, pain, or bodily health), but not including a statement of memory or belief to prove the fact remembered or believed unless it relates to the validity or terms of the declarant's will.

State of Mind:

- Present intent, motive, plan
- "I'm going to meet John tomorrow"
- "I hate my boss"

Physical/Emotional Condition:

- Present pain, illness, feelings
- "My back hurts"
- "I feel dizzy"

Key Limitation: Cannot use to prove past facts remembered.

Exception: Statements about wills (capacity, terms, validity).

Rule 803(4) - Statement Made for Medical Diagnosis or Treatment

A statement—made to a medical professional for the purpose of medical diagnosis or treatment and describing medical history, past or present symptoms or sensations, their inception, or their general cause.

Requirements:

- Made to medical professional
- For purpose of diagnosis or treatment
- Describes medical history, symptoms, sensations, or general cause

Scope:

- Includes statements to doctors, nurses, EMTs
- Past and present symptoms
- General causation ("I was hit by a car")
- Not specific fault ("John was speeding")

Child Abuse Context: Statements to social workers or therapists often admissible.

Rule 803(5) - Recorded Recollection

A record that:

(a) is on a matter the witness once knew about but now cannot recall well enough to testify fully and accurately;

(b) was made or adopted by the witness when the matter was fresh in the witness's memory; and

(c) accurately reflects the witness's knowledge.

If admitted, the record may be read into evidence but may not itself be received as an exhibit unless offered by an adverse party.

Requirements:

- Witness has insufficient present recollection
- Record made when memory was fresh
- Record accurately reflected knowledge at time made
- Proper foundation laid

Distinguished from Refreshing Recollection: Here witness still cannot remember; in refreshing, witness remembers after seeing document.

Limitation: Record read to jury, not admitted as exhibit (unless opponent offers it).

Rule 803(6) - Records of a Regularly Conducted Activity (Business Records)

A record of an act, event, condition, opinion, or diagnosis if:

(a) the record was made at or near the time by—or from information transmitted by—someone with knowledge;

(b) the record was kept in the course of a regularly conducted activity of a business, organization, occupation, or calling, whether or not for profit;

(c) making the record was a regular practice of that activity;

(d) all these conditions are shown by the testimony of the custodian or another qualified witness, or by a certification under Rule 902(11) or (12); and

(e) the opponent does not show that the source of information or the method or circumstances of preparation indicate a lack of trustworthiness.

Foundation Requirements:

1. Regular business activity

2. Regular practice to make such records

3. Made at or near time of event

4. Source had knowledge (personal or from someone with duty to report)

5. Proper witness (custodian or qualified witness)

6. Trustworthy (opponent cannot show lack of trustworthiness)

Scope: Very broad - includes medical records, corporate documents, computer records, etc.

Common Problems:

- Records prepared for litigation (trustworthiness issue)
- Multiple hearsay layers
- Source of information lacks business duty

Rule 803(7) - Absence of a Record of a Regularly Conducted Activity

Evidence that a matter is not included in a record described in Rule 803(6) if:

(a) the evidence is admitted to prove that the matter did not occur or exist;

(b) a record was regularly made for matters of that kind; and

(c) the conditions in Rule 803(6) are met.

Use: Prove non-occurrence of event by showing absence from business records.

Example: No record of payment in company's accounting records to prove payment was not made.

Rule 803(8) - Public Records

A record or statement of a public office if:

(a) it sets out:

(i) the office's activities;

(ii) a matter observed while under a legal duty to report, but not including, in a criminal case, a matter observed by law-enforcement personnel; or

(iii) in a civil case or against the government in a criminal case, factual findings from a legally authorized investigation; and

(b) the opponent does not show that the source of information or other circumstances indicate a lack of trustworthiness.

Three Categories:

Category A(i) - Office Activities:

- Routine governmental activities
- Birth certificates, marriage licenses, court records

Category A(ii) - Matters Observed:

- Public officials observing events under legal duty
- Weather records, inspection reports
- Criminal Case Limitation: Cannot use against defendant if observed by law enforcement

Category A(iii) - Investigative Findings:

- Results of official investigations
- Civil cases: Broadly admissible
- Criminal cases: Only against government, not defendant

Rule 803(10) - Absence of a Public Record

Testimony—or a certification under Rule 902—that a diligent search failed to disclose a public record or statement if:

(a) the testimony or certification is admitted to prove that

(i) the record or statement does not exist; or

(ii) a matter did not occur or exist, if a public office regularly made records or statements for matters of that kind; and

(b) the testimony or certification is by a public official or an officer or employee with sufficient knowledge of how records are kept and searched.

Use: Prove non-existence of records or non-occurrence of events.

Rule 803(18) - Learned Treatises

A statement contained in a treatise, periodical, or pamphlet if:

(a) the statement is called to the attention of an expert witness on cross-examination or relied on by the expert on direct examination; and

(b) the publication is established as a reliable authority by the expert's admission or testimony, by another expert's testimony, or by judicial notice.

Requirements:

- Must be called to expert's attention or relied upon by expert
- Must be established as reliable authority
- Can be used on direct or cross-examination

Limitation: Statement may be read to jury but treatise not admitted as exhibit.

Additional Rule 803 Exceptions (Brief Overview)

1. 803(9) - Records of Vital Statistics: Birth, death, marriage records.
2. 803(11) - Records of Religious Organizations: Baptisms, marriages, etc.
3. 803(12) - Certificates of Marriage, Baptism, etc.

4. 803(13) - Family Records: Genealogical information in family documents.
5. 803(14) - Records of Documents That Affect an Interest in Property
6. 803(15) - Statements in Documents That Affect Property Interest
7. 803(16) - Statements in Ancient Documents: Documents 20+ years old.
8. 803(17) - Market Reports and Similar Commercial Publications
9. 803(19) - Reputation Concerning Personal or Family History
10. 803(20) - Reputation Concerning Boundaries or General History
11. 803(21) - Reputation Concerning Character: When character in issue.
12. 803(22) - Judgment of Previous Conviction: Criminal convictions for impeachment and civil cases.
13. 803(23) - Judgments Involving Personal, Family, or General History

RULE 804. EXCEPTIONS TO THE RULE AGAINST HEARSAY—WHEN THE DECLARANT IS UNAVAILABLE AS A WITNESS

A. Criteria for Being Unavailable

A declarant is considered to be unavailable as a witness if the declarant:

(1) is exempted from testifying about the subject matter by a ruling on privilege;

(2) refuses to testify about the subject matter despite a court order;

(3) testifies to not remembering the subject matter;

(4) cannot be present or testify at the trial or hearing because of death or a then-existing infirmity, physical illness, or mental illness; or

(5) is absent from the trial or hearing and the statement's proponent has not been able, by process or other reasonable means, to procure the declarant's attendance or testimony.

But this subdivision (a) does not apply if the statement's proponent procured or wrongfully caused the declarant's unavailability.

Understanding Unavailability

Five Categories:

1. Privilege: Valid privilege claim prevents testimony

2. Refusal: Contempt-level refusal despite court order

3. Memory Loss: Claims inability to remember (tested by court)

4. Physical/Mental Incapacity: Death, illness, mental condition

5. Absence: Cannot locate or procure attendance despite reasonable efforts

Forfeiture: Cannot create unavailability through wrongdoing.

Rule 804(b)(1) - Former Testimony

Testimony that:

(a) was given as a witness at a trial, hearing, or lawful deposition, whether given during the current proceeding or a different one; and

(b) is now offered against a party who had—or, in a civil case, whose predecessor in interest had—an opportunity and similar motive to develop it by direct, cross-, or redirect examination.

Requirements:

- Prior testimony under oath
- Opportunity and similar motive to examine
- Against party who had that opportunity (or predecessor in interest in civil cases)

"Similar Motive" Test: Must have had similar reasons to examine witness in similar manner.

Predecessor in Interest: Civil cases allow broader application to parties in similar positions.

RULE 804(B)(2) - STATEMENT UNDER THE BELIEF OF IMMINENT DEATH

In a prosecution for homicide or in a civil case, a statement that the declarant, while believing the declarant's death to be imminent, made about its cause or circumstances.

Requirements:

- Belief death is imminent
- Statement about cause or circumstances of impending death
- Homicide prosecutions or civil cases (not other criminal cases)

Rationale: Assumption people don't lie when they think they're dying.

Modern Expansion: No longer requires declarant actually died.

Rule 804(b)(3) - Statement Against Interest

A statement that:

(a) a reasonable person in the declarant's position would have made only if the person believed it to be true because, when made, it was so contrary to the declarant's proprietary or pecuniary interest or had so great a tendency to invalidate the declarant's claim against someone else or to expose the declarant to civil or criminal liability; and

(b) is supported by corroborating circumstances that clearly indicate its trustworthiness, if it is offered in a criminal case and tends to expose the declarant to criminal liability.

Types of Statements Against Interest:

- Pecuniary: Against financial interest
- Proprietary: Against property interest
- Civil Liability: Subjects to lawsuit
- Criminal Liability: Subjects to criminal prosecution

Key Requirements:

- Must be against interest when made
- Reasonable person would only make if believed true
- Criminal cases: need corroborating circumstances for statements exposing criminal liability

Distinguished from Party Admissions: This requires unavailable non-party declarant; party admissions are always admissible against parties.

Rule 804(b)(6) - Statement Offered Against a Party That Wrongfully Caused the Declarant's Unavailability

A statement offered against a party that wrongfully caused—or acquiesced in wrongfully causing—the declarant's unavailability as a witness, and did so intending that result.

Forfeiture by Wrongdoing: Party who wrongfully makes declarant unavailable cannot object to hearsay.

Requirements:

- Wrongful conduct by party
- Caused declarant's unavailability
- Intent to make declarant unavailable

Common Application: Defendant intimidates or murders witness to prevent testimony.

RULE 805. HEARSAY WITHIN HEARSAY

Hearsay within hearsay is not admissible unless each part of the combined statements conforms with an exception to the hearsay rule.

Multiple Hearsay Analysis

Rule: Each level of hearsay must have its own exception.

Example: Hospital record containing patient's statement about accident.

- Level 1: Patient's statement to nurse (803(4) - medical treatment)
- Level 2: Nurse's recording in hospital record (803(6) - business record)

Common Problems:

- Business records containing witness statements
- Police reports with victim/witness statements
- Medical records with family member statements

Analysis Method: Identify each declarant and each statement, then find exception for each level.

RULE 806. ATTACKING AND SUPPORTING THE DECLARANT'S CREDIBILITY

When a hearsay statement—or a statement described in Rule 801(d)(2)(C), (D), or (E)—has been admitted in evidence, the declarant's credibility may be attacked, and then supported, by any evidence that would be admissible for those purposes if the declarant had testified as a witness. Evidence of the declarant's inconsistent statement or conduct is admissible only if the declarant has been afforded an opportunity to explain or deny the statement or conduct, and an adverse party has been afforded an opportunity to examine the declarant about it—or if justice so requires.

Impeaching Hearsay Declarants

General Rule: Can impeach hearsay declarant same as if they testified.

Methods Available:

- Character for truthfulness
- Prior convictions
- Bias evidence
- Prior inconsistent statements

Special Rule for Prior Inconsistent Statements: Must give declarant opportunity to explain/deny (unless justice requires otherwise).

RULE 807. RESIDUAL EXCEPTION

A. In General.

Under the following circumstances, a hearsay statement is not excluded by the rule against hearsay even if the statement is not specifically covered by a hearsay exception in Rule 803 or 804:

(1) the statement has equivalent circumstantial guarantees of trustworthiness;

(2) it is offered as evidence of a material fact;

(3) it is more probative on the point for which it is offered than any other evidence that the proponent can procure through reasonable efforts; and

(4) admitting it will best serve the purposes of these rules and the interests of justice.

B. Notice.

The statement is admissible only if, before the trial or hearing, the proponent gives an adverse party reasonable notice of the intent to offer the statement and its particulars, including the declarant's name and address, so that the party has a fair opportunity to meet it.

The Catch-All Exception

Four Requirements:

1. Equivalent guarantees of trustworthiness

2. Material fact

3. More probative than other available evidence

4. Serves interests of justice

Plus: Advance notice required

Purpose: Safety valve for trustworthy hearsay not covered by specific exceptions.

Rare Application: Courts reluctant to expand beyond enumerated exceptions.

HEARSAY STRATEGY AND COMMON ISSUES

Systematic Hearsay Analysis

Step 1: Identify the Statement

- What exactly is being offered?
- Who made the statement?
- When and where was it made?

Step 2: Hearsay Analysis

- Out-of-court statement?
- Offered for truth of matter asserted?
- If yes to both = hearsay

Step 3: Non-Hearsay Uses

- Effect on listener?
- Verbal act?
- State of mind of speaker?
- Impeachment?

Step 4: Exclusions (Rule 801(d))

- Prior statement by witness?
- Opposing party statement?

Step 5: Exceptions

- Rule 803 (availability immaterial)?
- Rule 804 (declarant unavailable)?
- Rule 807 (residual)?

Step 6: Multiple Hearsay

- Are there layers of hearsay?
- Does each level have an exception?

Common Hearsay Traps

Police Reports: Often contain multiple levels of hearsay - analyze each statement separately.

Medical Records: May contain family member statements not covered by medical treatment exception.

Business Records: Must establish all foundation elements; litigation-prepared records may lack trustworthiness.

Present Sense Impression vs. Excited Utterance: Time and excitement factors determine which applies.

State of Mind Exception: Cannot use to prove past facts remembered, only present mental state.

Strategic Considerations

For Proponents:

- Identify strongest exception available
- Prepare proper foundation witnesses
- Consider multiple exceptions for same statement
- Address multiple hearsay issues

For Opponents:

- Challenge each element of claimed exception
- Attack foundation requirements
- Argue alternative non-hearsay purposes
- Consider Rule 403 exclusion even if exception applies

Key Exam Points

Most Tested Exceptions:

- Present sense impression (803(1))
- Excited utterance (803(2))
- State of mind (803(3))
- Business records (803(6))
- Prior statements by witness (801(d)(1))
- Party admissions (801(d)(2))

Common Essay Issues:

- Multiple hearsay analysis
- Business record foundations
- Party admission subcategories
- State of mind exception limitations

Multiple Choice Favorites:

- Hearsay definition and non-truth uses
- Prior inconsistent statement requirements
- Co-conspirator statement elements
- Medical treatment exception scope

Final Reminder: Hearsay is a rule of exclusion with many exceptions. Always analyze systematically: definition first, then exclusions, then exceptions. Master the most common exceptions and understand their policy rationales for effective application.

ARTICLE IX – AUTHENTICATION AND IDENTIFICATION

Authentication requires establishing that evidence is what its proponent claims it to be before admission. Rule 901 provides multiple methods ranging from witness testimony to distinctive characteristics analysis. Rule 902 identifies categories of self-authenticating evidence. This foundational requirement applies to all physical evidence, documents, and recorded materials.

The foundation requirement - proving that evidence is what you claim it to be. Essential for all physical and documentary evidence.

RULE 901. AUTHENTICATING OR IDENTIFYING EVIDENCE

A. In General

To satisfy the requirement of authenticating or identifying an item of evidence, the proponent must produce evidence sufficient to support a finding that the item is what the proponent claims it to be.

(b) Examples

The following are examples only—not a complete list—of evidence that satisfies the requirement:

(1) Testimony of a Witness with Knowledge. Testimony that an item is what it is claimed to be.

(2) Nonexpert Opinion About Handwriting. A nonexpert's opinion that handwriting is genuine, based on a familiarity with it that was not acquired for the current litigation.

(3) Comparison by an Expert Witness or the Trier of Fact. A comparison with an authenticated specimen by an expert witness or the trier of fact.

(4) Distinctive Characteristics and the Like. The appearance, contents, substance, internal patterns, or other distinctive characteristics of the item, taken together with all the circumstances.

(5) Opinion About a Voice. An opinion identifying a person's voice, whether heard firsthand or through mechanical or electronic transmission or recording, based on hearing the voice at any time under circumstances that connect it with the alleged speaker.

(6) Evidence About a Phone Conversation. For a phone conversation, evidence that a call was made to the number assigned at the time to a particular person or business, with appropriate circumstances showing the connection.

(7) Evidence About Public Records. Evidence that a document was recorded or filed in a public office as authorized by law, or

that a purported public record was received from the public office where items of this kind are kept.

(8) Evidence About Ancient Documents. For documents at least 20 years old, evidence that the document is in good condition, was found in proper custody, and creates no suspicion about authenticity.

(9) Evidence About a Process or System. Evidence describing a process or system and showing that it produces an accurate result.

UNDERSTANDING AUTHENTICATION - THE FOUNDATION

The Basic Standard

Authentication = Enough Evidence to Support Finding that Item Is What Proponent Claims

Key Points:

- Low threshold: "sufficient to support a finding"
- Not proof beyond reasonable doubt or preponderance
- Judge makes preliminary determination under Rule 104(b)
- Goes to admissibility, not weight
- Authentication does not guarantee accuracy of contents

Rule 104(b) Standard

Conditional Relevance:

- Judge determines if reasonable jury could find item authentic
- If yes, evidence admitted and jury decides actual authentic
- Proponent need not prove authenticity conclusively

Authentication vs. Other Issues

Important Distinctions:

- Authentication: Is this the item claimed?
- Accuracy: Is the content true?
- Hearsay: Is out-of-court statement offered for truth?
- Best Evidence: Is original required?

KEY AUTHENTICATION METHODS

Rule 901(b)(1) - Testimony of Witness with Knowledge

Most Common Method: Witness testifies item is what it's claimed to be.

Requirements:

- Personal knowledge of the item
- Ability to identify it at trial
- Foundation establishing how witness knows

Examples:

- "This is the contract I signed with defendant"

- "This photograph accurately shows the accident scene as I saw it"
- "This is the gun I saw defendant holding"

Chain of Custody: Critical for physical evidence to show no tampering.

Foundation Elements:

- Who collected evidence and when
- How stored and by whom
- Who had access
- Witness can identify at trial

Rule 901(b)(2) - Nonexpert Handwriting Opinion

Lay Opinion Requirements:

- Witness familiar with person's handwriting
- Familiarity not acquired for current litigation
- Sufficient basis to form opinion

Sources of Proper Familiarity:

- Regular correspondence
- Business relationship involving signed documents
- Observing person sign documents
- Family relationship with document exchanges

Excluded: Cannot become familiar specifically to testify.

Rule 901(b)(4) - Distinctive Characteristics

Circumstantial Authentication: Internal evidence shows authenticity.

Common Applications:

Reply Letter Doctrine:

- Letter responds to earlier correspondence
- References specific facts from prior letter
- Shows knowledge only true recipient would have

Content Knowledge:

- Document contains facts only authentic author would know
- Internal consistency with other authenticated documents
- References to private conversations or events

Business Documents:

- Consistent letterhead and formatting
- Internal reference numbers
- Standard business language and procedures

Rule 901(b)(5) - Voice Identification

Requirements:

- Witness heard voice before under circumstances connecting it to alleged speaker
- Can be live conversation, phone call, or recording

- No minimum familiarity period required

Scope:

- Previous face-to-face conversations
- Prior telephone calls
- Recorded statements
- Electronic transmissions

Note: Even brief prior contact may suffice if provides adequate basis for identification.

Rule 901(b)(6) - Phone Conversations

Two Categories:

Personal Calls:

- Call made to number assigned to particular person
- Circumstances show person answering was the one called
- May include self-identification, voice recognition, knowledge of facts

Business Calls:

- Call made to business number
- Conversation related to business reasonably transacted by phone
- More liberal - presumes person answering represents business

Rule 901(b)(8) - Ancient Documents

Three Requirements:

1. Document at least 20 years old when offered

2. In condition creating no suspicion about authenticity

3. Found in place where authentic document would likely be kept

Rationale: Age and proper custody create inference of authenticity.

Examples:

- Old deed found in property owner's safe
- Family Bible with birth records found in family home
- Corporate records in company files

Rule 901(b)(9) - Process or System

For Generated Evidence: Must show process/system produces accurate results.

Common Applications:

- Computer printouts and records
- Automated camera systems (red light, speed cameras)
- Scientific testing equipment
- Telephone and communication systems
- ATM and banking records

Foundation Requirements:

- Description of process or system
- Evidence system produces accurate results
- System operating properly at relevant time
- Qualified operator if human involvement required

RULE 902. EVIDENCE THAT IS SELF-AUTHENTICATING

No extrinsic evidence of authenticity required - but can still be challenged.

Key Categories

(1) Sealed and Signed Government Documents

- Documents bearing official government seal and signature
- Federal, state, local government documents
- Includes agencies and political subdivisions

(4) Certified Copies of Public Records

- Official records certified by custodian
- Alternative to producing originals
- Certification must comply with applicable requirements

(5) Official Publications

- Government-issued publications
- Statutes, regulations, agency reports

- Books, pamphlets from public authorities

(6) Newspapers and Periodicals

- Published newspapers and magazines
- No additional proof of publication needed
- Establishes publication, not accuracy of contents

(7) Trade Inscriptions

- Labels, tags, signs indicating origin, ownership, control
- Must be affixed in course of business
- Product labels, manufacturer marks, brand names

(8) Acknowledged Documents

- Documents with proper notarization
- Certificate of acknowledgment by authorized officer
- Notary public or other authorized official

(11) Certified Business Records (Domestic)

- Records meeting Rule 803(6) requirements
- Custodian certification under federal statute or Supreme Court rule
- Advance notice required to opponent
- Must make available for inspection

Important: Self-authentication establishes prima facie authenticity but evidence can still be challenged.

RULE 903. SUBSCRIBING WITNESS'S TESTIMONY

Modern rule: Subscribing witness testimony generally not required unless governing jurisdiction's law specifically requires it.

Limited applications remain for certain wills and formal documents under state law.

AUTHENTICATION STRATEGY AND COMMON ISSUES

Electronic Evidence Authentication

Growing Area of Practice:

Email Messages:

- Distinctive characteristics (writing style, knowledge of facts)
- Reply chains showing context
- Header information and metadata
- Witness testimony about sending/receiving

Text Messages:

- Phone records showing message traffic
- Screenshots with proper foundation
- Witness testimony about conversations
- Reply patterns and context

Computer Records:

- System reliability under Rule 901(b)(9)

- Regular maintenance and operation
- Access controls and security measures
- Witness testimony about business practices

Photographs and Videos

Foundation Requirements:

- Witness can testify image accurately depicts what it purports to show
- Taken at relevant time
- No material alterations
- Chain of custody for originals

Digital Images:

- Metadata can provide authentication evidence
- Consider enhancement or editing issues
- Witness testimony about taking photograph
- Camera system reliability for automated systems

Common Strategic Considerations

For Proponents:

- Choose most efficient authentication method available
- Consider multiple methods for important evidence
- Prepare backup authentication if primary method fails
- Establish chain of custody early and thoroughly
- Use self-authentication when possible

For Opponents:

- Challenge each element of authentication foundation
- Question gaps in chain of custody
- Present evidence of alteration or tampering
- Attack witness qualifications or memory
- Distinguish authentication from accuracy issues

Frequent Exam Issues

1. Multiple Authentication Methods: Can use several approaches together.
2. Authentication vs. Hearsay: Separate inquiries - authentication establishes identity, hearsay rules govern admissibility of contents.
3. Electronic Evidence: Understand system reliability requirements and modern digital evidence issues.
4. Chain of Custody: Critical for physical evidence, especially controlled substances and weapons.
5. Ancient Documents: Remember all three requirements (age, condition, custody).
6. Self-Authentication Limitations: Prima facie only - can be rebutted.

Key Principle: Authentication is a relatively low threshold designed to let the jury decide ultimate questions of authenticity and weight. Focus on establishing sufficient evidence of identity, not proving conclusively that evidence is genuine.

Article X – Contents of Writings, Recordings, and Photographs

The Best Evidence Rule requires production of original documents when their contents are material to the case. Rules 1003-1004 establish exceptions permitting duplicates and secondary evidence under specific circumstances. Rule 1006 governs the use of summaries for voluminous records. This rule applies only when document contents are actually disputed.

The "Best Evidence Rule" - when you want to prove what a document says, you generally need the original document.

RULE 1001. DEFINITIONS THAT APPLY TO THIS ARTICLE

Writings and Recordings

"Writings" and "recordings" consist of letters, words, numbers, or their equivalent set down in any form.

Photographs

"Photographs" include still photographs, X-ray films, video tapes, and motion pictures.

Original

An "original" of a writing or recording means the writing or recording itself or any counterpart intended to have the same effect by the person who executed or issued it.

For electronically stored information, an "original" means any printout—or other output readable by sight—if it accurately reflects the information.

Duplicate

A "duplicate" means a counterpart produced by a mechanical, photographical, chemical, electronic, or other equivalent process or technique that accurately reproduces the original.

RULE 1002. REQUIREMENT OF THE ORIGINAL

An original writing, recording, or photograph is required in order to prove its contents unless these rules or a federal statute provides otherwise.

RULE 1003. ADMISSIBILITY OF DUPLICATES

A duplicate is admissible to the same extent as the original unless:

(1) a genuine question is raised about the original's authenticity; or

(2) the circumstances make it unfair to admit the duplicate.

RULE 1004. ADMISSIBILITY OF OTHER EVIDENCE OF CONTENT

An original is not required and other evidence of the content of a writing, recording, or photograph is admissible if:

(1) Originals Lost or Destroyed. All the originals are lost or have been destroyed, and not by the proponent acting in bad faith;

(2) Original Not Obtainable. An original cannot be obtained by any available judicial process or procedure;

(3) Original in Possession of Opponent. At a time when an original was under the control of the party against whom the original is now offered, that party was put on notice, by pleadings or otherwise, that the original would be a subject of proof at the trial or hearing, and that party does not produce it at the trial or hearing; or

(4) Collateral Matters. The writing, recording, or photograph is not closely related to a controlling issue.

RULE 1005. COPIES OF PUBLIC RECORDS TO PROVE CONTENT

The proponent may use a copy to prove the content of an official record—or of a document that was recorded or filed in a public office as authorized by law—if these conditions are met:

(1) the copy is certified as correct in accordance with Rule 902(4) or is testified to be correct by a witness who has compared it with the original; and

(2) the original or a duplicate is not shown to be available by the proponent's reasonable efforts.

RULE 1006. SUMMARIES TO PROVE CONTENT

The proponent may use a summary, chart, or calculation to prove the content of voluminous writings, recordings, or photographs that cannot be conveniently examined in court. The proponent must make the originals or duplicates available for examination or copying, or both, by other parties at a reasonable time and place. And the court may order the proponent to produce them in court.

RULE 1007. TESTIMONY OR STATEMENT OF A PARTY TO PROVE CONTENT

The proponent may prove the content of a writing, recording, or photograph by the testimony, deposition, or written statement of the party against whom the evidence is offered. The proponent need not account for the original.

RULE 1008. FUNCTIONS OF THE COURT AND JURY

Ordinarily, the court determines whether the proponent has fulfilled the factual conditions for admitting other evidence of the content of a writing, recording, or photograph under Rule

1004 or 1005. But in a jury trial, the jury determines—in accordance with Rule 104(b)—any issue about whether:

(a) an asserted writing, recording, or photograph ever existed;

(b) another one produced at the trial or hearing is the original; or

(c) other evidence of content accurately reflects the content.

UNDERSTANDING THE BEST EVIDENCE RULE

The Basic Principle

When Content Is at Issue: Must produce original writing, recording, or photograph to prove what it says.

Traditional Name: "Best Evidence Rule" - though modern rule is more accurately the "Original Document Rule."

Scope of Application

Rule Only Applies When:

- Proving contents of writing, recording, or photograph
- Content is material to the case
- Not when document merely mentioned or referenced

Key Question: Are you trying to prove what the document says, or just that it exists?

When Rule 1002 Applies

Document Contents in Issue:

- Contract terms in dispute
- Exact wording of will or deed
- Specific language in correspondence
- Amount stated in invoice or receipt

Document Contents Not in Issue:

- Witness saw defendant sign a contract (fact of signing)
- Photo was taken at accident scene (fact photo exists)
- Letter was mailed on certain date (fact of mailing)

Writings, Recordings, and Photographs Defined

Broad Scope Under Rule 1001:

- Traditional documents (contracts, letters, deeds)
- Electronic records (emails, text messages, databases)
- Audio recordings (conversations, phone calls)
- Video recordings (surveillance, depositions)
- X-rays and medical imaging
- Computer files and digital data

RULE 1001 DEFINITIONS - KEY CONCEPTS

What Constitutes an "Original"

Traditional Documents:

- The document itself as executed

- Counterparts intended to have same effect (multiple originals of contract)

Electronic Information:

- Any printout or output readable by sight
- Must accurately reflect the information
- Multiple "originals" possible for electronic data

Examples:

- Email printed from server = original
- Word document printed from computer = original
- Database report generated from system = original

What Constitutes a "Duplicate"

Rule 1003 Definition:

- Counterpart produced by mechanical, photographical, chemical, electronic, or equivalent process
- Must accurately reproduce the original

Common Examples:

- Photocopies
- Carbon copies
- Digital scans
- Fax transmissions
- Computer backup copies

Not Duplicates:

- Hand-copied documents

- Transcriptions
- Summaries or abstracts

Rule 1003 - Admissibility of Duplicates

General Rule

Duplicates admissible same as originals.

Two Exceptions:

Exception 1 - Authenticity Question:

- Genuine question raised about original's authenticity
- Suspicion of alteration or forgery
- Dispute about whether original ever existed

Exception 2 - Unfairness:

- Circumstances make duplicate admission unfair
- Quality issues preventing fair comparison
- Strategic disadvantage to opponent

Examples of Unfairness:

- Poor quality photocopy obscures critical details
- Duplicate missing pages or portions
- Color important but only black and white copy available

RULE 1004 - EXCEPTIONS TO ORIGINAL REQUIREMENT

Four Recognized Excuses

(1) Originals Lost or Destroyed

Requirements:

- All originals lost or destroyed
- Not destroyed by proponent in bad faith
- Reasonable search conducted

Good Faith Standard:

- Accidental loss or destruction acceptable
- Routine business destruction acceptable
- Intentional destruction to avoid litigation = bad faith

Foundation Required:

- Witness testimony about loss/destruction
- Evidence of search efforts
- Circumstances of loss

(2) Original Not Obtainable

Situations:

- Document in foreign country beyond subpoena power
- Third party refuses to produce despite court order
- Document in government possession and unavailable
- Original destroyed by natural disaster

Must Show:

- Attempts made to obtain original
- Available judicial process insufficient
- Not due to proponent's fault

(3) Original in Possession of Opponent

Requirements:

- Original was under opponent's control
- Opponent put on notice original would be needed
- Notice can be through pleadings or other means
- Opponent fails to produce at trial

Strategic Use:

- Request production in discovery
- Notice in pretrial motions
- Demand at trial
- If opponent fails to produce, can use secondary evidence

(4) Collateral Matters

Standard: Writing not closely related to controlling issue.

Examples:

- Receipt for minor expense in major contract dispute
- Routine correspondence in fraud case
- Background documents not central to claims

Balancing Test:

- Importance of document to case
- Difficulty of obtaining original
- Availability of other proof
- Prejudice to parties

RULE 1005 - PUBLIC RECORDS EXCEPTION

Special Rule for Government Documents

Rationale: Originals of public records should remain in official custody.

Requirements:

- Copy certified under Rule 902(4), OR
- Witness testifies copy is correct after comparison with original
- Original not shown available through reasonable efforts

Common Applications:

- Birth certificates
- Property records
- Court documents
- Government agency files

RULE 1006 - SUMMARIES OF VOLUMINOUS DOCUMENTS

When Summaries Allowed

Requirements:

- Documents are voluminous
- Cannot be conveniently examined in court
- Summary accurately reflects contents
- Underlying documents available for inspection

Foundation:

- Witness prepared summary or supervised preparation
- Witness reviewed underlying documents
- Summary accurately reflects contents
- No selective omission of unfavorable material

Procedure:

- Advance notice to opponents
- Make originals available for examination
- Court may order production in court
- Opponent can examine underlying documents

Common Uses:

- Financial records in fraud cases
- Medical records in malpractice
- Business records in commercial disputes
- Tax records in enforcement actions

RULE 1007 - PARTY ADMISSIONS EXCEPTION

Using Opponent's Own Testimony

Scope: Can prove document contents through opponent's testimony, deposition, or written statement.

Advantage: No need to account for original.

Applications:

- Opponent testifies about contract terms
- Deposition testimony about document contents
- Admissions in pleadings about what document said
- Interrogatory responses describing documents

Limitation: Only applies to party opponents, not third-party witnesses.

RULE 1008 - COURT AND JURY FUNCTIONS

Division of Responsibilities

Judge Decides (Rule 104(a)):

- Whether Rule 1004 or 1005 conditions met
- Admissibility of secondary evidence
- Preliminary factual determinations

Jury Decides (Rule 104(b)):

- Whether asserted document ever existed
- Whether produced document is the original
- Whether secondary evidence accurately reflects content

Practical Impact

Conditional Admissibility:

- Judge admits secondary evidence if conditions arguably met
- Jury decides ultimate questions about accuracy and authenticity
- Weight and credibility remain jury questions

STRATEGIC CONSIDERATIONS AND COMMON ISSUES

Planning and Discovery

For Documents You Need:

- Request originals in discovery
- Identify all sources of copies
- Prepare foundation for any Rule 1004 exceptions'
- Consider summary evidence for voluminous records

For Documents Opponent Needs:

- Preserve originals carefully
- Consider strategic advantages of requiring originals
- Prepare challenges to secondary evidence
- Examine quality of duplicates

Electronic Evidence Issues

Modern Applications:

- Email printouts generally qualify as originals
- Database reports are originals if accurately reflect data
- Text message screenshots need proper foundation
- Cloud storage creates multiple "originals"

Authentication vs. Best Evidence:

- Authentication: Is this the document claimed?
- Best Evidence: Is original required to prove contents?
- Often both issues arise with electronic evidence

Common Exam Scenarios

Contract Disputes:

- Exact terms in issue = need original
- Fact that contract was signed = original not required

Recorded Conversations:

- What was said = need original recording
- That conversation occurred = original not required

Photographs:

- Details shown in photo = need original
- That photo was taken = original not required

PRACTICAL APPLICATIONS

Foundation Requirements

For Rule 1004(1) - Lost/Destroyed:

1. Document once existed
2. Witness had knowledge of contents
3. All originals lost or destroyed
4. Loss not due to bad faith
5. Reasonable search conducted

For Rule 1004(3) - Opponent Possession:

1. Document was in opponent's control
2. Adequate notice given
3. Document relevant to case
4. Opponent failed to produce

For Rule 1006 - Summaries:

1. Documents are voluminous
2. Cannot be conveniently examined in court
3. Summary accurately reflects contents
4. Underlying documents available to opponent

Strategic Tips

Avoid Problems:

- Identify potential best evidence issues early
- Request document production comprehensively
- Preserve originals carefully
- Prepare alternative proof methods

Use Tactically:

- Force opponent to produce originals
- Challenge quality of duplicates when material
- Use summaries for complex financial data
- Leverage party admissions about document contents

Common Mistakes

Misunderstanding Scope:

- Rule only applies when proving contents
- Not when document merely referenced
- Distinguish from authentication requirements

Inadequate Foundation:

- Failing to show search efforts for lost documents
- Insufficient notice to opponent
- Poor foundation for summaries

Overlooking Exceptions:

- Not considering all Rule 1004 alternatives
- Missing opportunities for party admissions

- Failing to use public records exception

Key Takeaway: The Best Evidence Rule is narrower than often assumed - it only requires originals when document contents are actually in dispute. Focus on whether you're proving what the document says (contents) or just that it exists or was signed (fact of document).

ARTICLE XI— MISCELLANEOUS RULES

These final provisions define the scope and applicability of the Federal Rules of Evidence. Rule 1101 specifies covered courts and proceedings while establishing important exceptions for grand jury proceedings, sentencing, and preliminary determinations. The rules govern federal civil and criminal trials but have limited application to certain pretrial and post-trial proceedings.

Final provisions governing scope, amendments, and applicability of the Federal Rules of Evidence.

RULE 1101. APPLICABILITY OF THE RULES

(a) To Courts and Judges

These rules apply to proceedings before:

- United States district courts
- United States bankruptcy and magistrate judges
- United States courts of appeals
- United States Court of Federal Claims
- District courts of Guam, the Virgin Islands, and the Northern Mariana Islands

(b) To Cases and Proceedings

These rules apply in:

- civil cases and proceedings, including bankruptcy, admiralty, and maritime cases
- criminal cases and proceedings
- contempt proceedings, except those in which the court may act summarily

(c) Rules on Privilege

The rules on privilege apply to all stages of a case or proceeding.

(d) Exceptions

These rules—except for those on privilege—do not apply to the following:

(1) Preliminary Questions of Fact - Court's determination under Rule 104(a) whether evidence is admissible

(2) Grand Jury - Proceedings before grand juries

(3) Miscellaneous Criminal Proceedings - Including preliminary examinations, sentencing, probation, bail

(4) Summary Contempt - When court may act summarily

Understanding Rule 1101 - Scope and Applicability

Where Rules Apply

Federal Courts: All federal district courts, courts of appeals, bankruptcy courts, magistrate judges, Court of Federal Claims, and territorial courts.

Types of Cases: Civil and criminal cases, admiralty, bankruptcy, contempt proceedings (except summary contempt).

Key Exceptions

Rule 104(a) Determinations: When judge decides admissibility questions, evidence rules don't apply to that determination.

- Example: Judge can consider hearsay when deciding if witness is competent
- Judge can review inadmissible evidence to rule on objections

Grand Jury Proceedings: Evidence rules don't apply.

- Grand jury can consider hearsay, opinion testimony, etc.
- Different standard than trial proceedings

Sentencing: Evidence rules relaxed at sentencing.

- Hearsay commonly admitted
- Lower standard of proof
- Focus on rehabilitation and punishment factors

Privilege Rules Always Apply: Even in proceedings where other evidence rules don't apply, privilege protections remain.

Practical Impact

Trial vs. Pretrial: Most evidence rules apply only at trial and formal hearings, not to discovery or informal proceedings.

Summary Proceedings: Court may act on limited evidence in emergency situations without full evidence rule compliance.

RULE 1102. AMENDMENTS

These rules may be amended as provided in 28 U.S.C. § 2072.

Amendment Process

- Supreme Court proposes amendments
- Comment period and review process
- Congressional review period
- Automatic effectiveness unless Congress acts

Recent Trends

- Modernization for electronic evidence
- Clarification of existing rules
- Response to circuit splits
- Updates for technological changes

RULE 1103. TITLE

These rules may be cited as the Federal Rules of Evidence.

Key Concepts for Article XI

Scope Limitations

1. Federal Only: State courts have their own evidence rules (though many based on Federal Rules).
2. Civil and Criminal: Same rules generally apply to both, with specific criminal procedure modifications.
3. Privilege Exception: Privilege rules apply everywhere - discovery, grand jury (for testimonial privileges), sentencing, etc.

Common Exam Issues

Grand Jury Exception:

- Question: Can prosecutor use hearsay before grand jury?
- Answer: Yes, Rule 1101(d)(2) exception applies

Sentencing Exception:

- Question: Can judge consider inadmissible evidence at sentencing?
- Answer: Yes, Rule 1101(d)(3) allows relaxed evidence standards

Rule 104(a) Exception:

- Question: Can judge consider hearsay when ruling on admissibility?
- Answer: Yes, judge not bound by evidence rules for preliminary determinations

Strategic Considerations

Know Your Forum: Federal vs. state court rules may differ significantly.

Procedural Stage Matters: Evidence rules apply differently at trial vs. sentencing vs. preliminary proceedings.

Privilege Always Protects: Even when other evidence rules relaxed, privilege claims remain viable.

Practical Applications

Criminal Practice:

- Grand jury can hear any evidence
- Preliminary hearings have relaxed standards
- Sentencing allows broader evidence
- Trial requires full compliance with evidence rules

Civil Practice:

- Discovery not governed by admissibility rules
- Summary judgment motions may consider inadmissible evidence for limited purposes
- Trial requires full evidence rule compliance

Bankruptcy and Specialized Courts:

- Same federal evidence rules apply
- Some specialized procedures may have additional requirements

Final Note: Article XI provisions are rarely tested but important for understanding when and where evidence rules apply. Focus on the major exceptions: grand jury, sentencing, and Rule 104(a) determinations.

ADVISORY COMMITTEE NOTES

The Advisory Committee's explanatory comments reveal the "why" behind each evidence rule. These official insights from the rule drafters provide essential context for understanding policy rationales, intended applications, and practical considerations that courts rely on when interpreting the Federal Rules of Evidence.

RELEVANCE AND RULE 403 BALANCING

Rule 401 - Test for Relevant Evidence

1. Advisory Committee Insight: The standard for relevance is minimal - evidence need only have "any tendency" to make a fact more or less probable. The committee emphasized that relevance is not measured by the degree of probative force, but simply whether the evidence has any probative value at all.

2. Practical Application: The committee noted that relevance determinations should be made liberally, with close questions resolved in favor of admission. The rule was designed to avoid the rigid common law restrictions that excluded evidence with minimal probative value.

3. Modern Interpretation: The committee recognized that relevance must be evaluated in context. Evidence that seems

irrelevant in isolation may become highly relevant when considered with other evidence in the case.

Rule 403 - Excluding Relevant Evidence

Core Committee Guidance: Rule 403 provides the essential safety valve against relevant but problematic evidence. The committee emphasized that exclusion requires that probative value be "substantially outweighed" - a high standard favoring admission.

Balancing Factors: The committee identified key considerations:

- Unfair Prejudice: Distinguished from legitimate prejudice that flows from probative evidence
- Confusion of Issues: Evidence that sidetracks the jury from main issues
- Misleading the Jury: Evidence that suggests inferences not supported by logic
- Undue Delay: Cumulative evidence or time-consuming presentation
- Waste of Time: Marginal evidence requiring extensive foundation

Timing Considerations: The committee noted that Rule 403 balancing should consider the time and attention the evidence will require relative to its importance to the case.

Trial Court Discretion: The committee emphasized that Rule 403 determinations are highly fact-specific and within the trial court's discretion, making appellate reversal difficult.

CHARACTER EVIDENCE

Rule 404(a) - Character to Prove Conduct

1. Committee's Policy Rationale: The general prohibition reflects the committee's view that character evidence creates substantial risk of unfair prejudice and confusion. People should be judged on what they did, not who they are generally perceived to be.

2. Criminal Case Exceptions: The committee recognized special considerations in criminal cases where defendants face loss of liberty. Defendants may present pertinent character evidence, and prosecution may respond in kind. The "mercy rule" allows defendants to present good character evidence.

3. Victim Character: When self-defense is claimed, the committee noted that victim's character for violence becomes relevant to whether victim was likely the aggressor.

Rule 404(b) - Other Crimes, Wrongs, or Acts

1. Committee Emphasis: This rule prohibits character evidence but permits evidence of other acts for specific, articulated purposes. The committee stressed that prosecutors must identify the specific non-propensity purpose before admission.

2. MIMIC Purposes: The committee provided guidance on common permissible purposes:

- Motive: Why defendant committed the charged act
- Intent: Defendant's state of mind, absence of mistake
- Mistake: Rebutting claim of innocent mistake

- Identity: Distinctive method or signature
- Common Plan: Evidence of larger scheme

3. Timing and Similarity: The committee noted that other acts need not be identical to charged conduct, but must be sufficiently similar to support the claimed inference. Temporal proximity increases probative value but is not required.

Rule 405 - Methods of Proving Character

1. Committee Guidance on Reputation: The committee preferred reputation evidence over opinion evidence, viewing community reputation as more reliable than individual opinions. However, both are permitted under the modern rule.

2. Specific Acts Limitation: The committee was concerned about the time-consuming nature of proving specific acts and the risk of confusion. Specific acts are generally limited to cross-examination of character witnesses.

IMPEACHMENT AND WITNESS CREDIBILITY

Rule 607 - Who May Impeach

1. Committee's Modern Approach: The traditional rule prohibiting impeachment of one's own witness was abolished. The committee recognized that parties should not be stuck with unexpected or hostile witness testimony.

2. Limitations: While any party may impeach any witness, the committee noted that courts retain authority under Rule 403

to prevent abuse, such as calling a witness solely to impeach them with prior statements.

Rule 608 - Character for Truthfulness

1. Committee Balance: The rule reflects the committee's balance between allowing credibility challenges and preventing character assassinations. Reputation and opinion evidence are permitted, but specific acts are generally excluded except on cross-examination.

2. Rehabilitation Timing: The committee emphasized that character for truthfulness can only be rehabilitated after it has been attacked. This prevents parties from bolstering witness credibility preemptively.

3. Specific Acts on Cross: The committee allowed inquiries about specific acts probative of truthfulness but required good faith basis and court discretion to prevent harassment.

Rule 609 - Criminal Convictions

1. Committee's Balancing Approach: The rule reflects extensive committee debate about balancing probative value against prejudicial effect. The committee recognized that criminal convictions have high probative value for credibility but create significant prejudice risks.

2. Felony Convictions: The committee established a presumption favoring admission of felonies less than 10 years

old, but required special balancing for criminal defendants to protect their right to testify.

3. Crimes of Dishonesty: The committee determined that convictions involving dishonesty or false statement are always admissible because they directly relate to truthfulness, regardless of whether they are felonies.

4. Time Limitations: The 10-year rule reflects the committee's judgment that older convictions lose probative value and increase prejudicial effect over time.

EXPERT TESTIMONY AND SCIENTIFIC EVIDENCE

Rule 701 - Lay Opinion Testimony

1. Committee Distinction: The committee drew a clear line between lay opinion based on perception and expert testimony based on scientific or technical knowledge. Lay witnesses may offer opinions that are helpful shortcuts to describing observations.

2. Common Examples: The committee endorsed lay opinions about speed, intoxication, emotional state, and similar matters within common experience. However, lay witnesses cannot offer opinions requiring specialized knowledge.

Rule 702 - Expert Testimony

1. Committee Standards: The committee established four requirements for expert testimony: qualified expert, reliable

methodology, reliable application, and helpfulness to trier of fact.

2. Reliability Focus: Following Daubert, the committee emphasized that judges must act as gatekeepers, ensuring that expert testimony is based on reliable principles and methods rather than mere speculation.

3. Helpfulness Standard: The committee noted that expert testimony must assist the trier of fact rather than simply restating common knowledge or invading the jury's province on ultimate legal conclusions.

Rule 703 - Basis of Expert Opinion

1. Committee's Practical Approach: Experts may rely on inadmissible evidence if reasonably relied upon by experts in the field. This recognizes that experts routinely base opinions on hearsay and other inadmissible evidence in their professional work.

2. Disclosure Limitations: The committee later added restrictions on disclosing the underlying inadmissible evidence to prevent circumventing hearsay rules. Such evidence may be disclosed only if probative value substantially outweighs prejudicial effect.

HEARSAY EXCEPTIONS AND RELIABILITY

Rule 801 - Hearsay Definition and Exclusions

1. Committee's Analytical Framework: The committee defined hearsay functionally based on the hearsay dangers: lack of oath, inability to observe demeanor, and absence of cross-examination. Statements not offered for truth avoid these dangers.

2. Prior Statements: The committee created exclusions for certain prior statements by witnesses who testify and are subject to cross-examination, reasoning that current cross-examination can test the reliability of prior statements.

3. Party Admissions: The committee excluded party admissions from hearsay based on adversary system principles - parties should not be able to object to their own statements being used against them.

Rule 803 - Exceptions Regardless of Availability

1. Committee's Reliability Theory: Each exception is based on circumstantial guarantees of trustworthiness that substitute for the usual safeguards of oath, demeanor, and cross-examination.

2. Present Sense Impression (803(1)): The committee emphasized that spontaneity reduces the likelihood of fabrication. The contemporaneous nature of the statement provides reliability.

3. Excited Utterance (803(2)): The committee found that the stress of excitement eliminates the possibility of reflective self-interest that might produce fabrication.

4. State of Mind (803(3)): The committee noted high reliability when people describe their current mental, emotional, or physical condition, but excluded statements of memory or belief about past facts.

5. Medical Treatment (803(4)): The committee recognized that people have strong incentives to be truthful when seeking medical care. The exception extends to statements about general causation but not specific fault.

6. Business Records (803(6)): The committee emphasized that the routine nature of business record-keeping, combined with business incentives for accuracy, provides reliability. The exception requires that record-making be a regular practice and that sources have a business duty to report accurately.

7. Public Records (803(8)): The committee found that official duties and public accountability provide reliability guarantees. However, the committee limited use against criminal defendants to protect confrontation rights.

Rule 804 - Exceptions When Declarant Unavailable

1. Committee's Necessity Theory: These exceptions require both reliability indicators and necessity (unavailability of declarant).

2. Former Testimony (804(b)(1)): The committee required that the party against whom testimony is offered had

opportunity and similar motive to examine the witness, ensuring adequate confrontation occurred.

3. Statement Against Interest (804(b)(3)): The committee found that people generally do not make statements harmful to their interests unless true. The exception requires that reasonable persons would not make such statements unless they believed them true.

AUTHENTICATION AND BEST EVIDENCE

Rule 901 - Authentication Requirements

1. Committee's Practical Standard: The committee established a low threshold for authentication - evidence sufficient to support a finding of authenticity. This allows the jury to determine ultimate authenticity questions while ensuring minimal foundation requirements are met.

2. Modern Technology: The committee recognized that authentication methods must evolve with technology. The examples in Rule 901(b) are illustrative, not exhaustive, allowing courts to adapt to new forms of evidence.

3. Distinctive Characteristics: The committee endorsed circumstantial authentication through distinctive characteristics, recognizing that modern business practices often provide internal evidence of authenticity.

Rule 902 - Self-Authentication

1. Committee Efficiency: The committee identified categories of evidence with such high inherent reliability that no extrinsic authentication evidence is required. This promotes efficiency while maintaining accuracy.

2. Government Documents: The committee found that official seals and signatures provide sufficient guarantees of authenticity for government documents.

3. Business Records: The committee later added provisions for certified business records to promote efficiency in commercial litigation while requiring advance notice to ensure fairness.

Rule 1002 - Original Document Rule

1. Committee's Limited Scope: The committee clarified that the Best Evidence Rule applies only when document contents are in issue, not when documents are merely mentioned or their existence is relevant.

2. Electronic Records: The committee adapted the rule for modern technology, recognizing that electronic information may have multiple "originals" and that printouts constitute originals if they accurately reflect the data.

KEY ADVISORY COMMITTEE THEMES

Balancing Approach

The committee consistently balanced probative value against potential harm, preferring admission with safeguards over exclusion.

Modernization

The committee regularly updated rules to address technological changes and evolving legal practices while maintaining core reliability principles.

Practical Application

The committee emphasized workable standards that trial courts can apply consistently rather than rigid formalistic requirements.

Adversary System Support

The committee designed rules to support the adversary system while protecting against unfair advantage and ensuring reliable fact-finding.

Judicial Discretion

The committee provided frameworks for judicial decision-making while preserving necessary flexibility for case-specific determinations.

Note: These insights represent the most practically significant Advisory Committee guidance for understanding and applying the Federal Rules of Evidence. The committee's explanations provide crucial context for interpreting rules and understanding their policy foundations.

QUICK REVIEW AND PRACTICE

MOST TESTED RULES SUMMARY

Article IV - Relevance (Rules 401-415)

1. Rule 401 - Relevant Evidence: Has tendency to make fact more/less probable + fact is of consequence.

2. Rule 403 - Prejudicial Evidence: Exclude if probative value substantially outweighed by unfair prejudice, confusion, misleading jury, delay, or waste of time.

3. Rule 404(a) - Character Evidence: Generally inadmissible to prove conduct. Exceptions: defendant opens door in criminal cases; victim character when self-defense claimed.

4. Rule 404(b) - Other Acts: Not admissible to prove character/propensity. Admissible for MIMIC: Motive, Intent, Mistake (absence of), Identity, Common plan/scheme.

5. Rule 407 - Subsequent Remedial Measures: Inadmissible to prove negligence or defect. Admissible to prove ownership, control, feasibility, or impeachment.

6. Rule 408 - Compromise Negotiations: Inadmissible to prove liability or amount. Must be claim disputed in good faith.

Article VI - Witnesses (Rules 601-615)

1. Rule 602 - Personal Knowledge: Witness must have personal knowledge of matters testified about.

2. Rule 607 - Impeachment: Any party may impeach any witness.

3. Rule 608 - Character for Truthfulness: Can attack with reputation/opinion evidence. Can only rehabilitate after attack. No specific instances except on cross of character witness.

4. Rule 609 - Criminal Convictions: Felonies less than 10 years old generally admissible. Crimes of dishonesty always admissible. Balancing test for criminal defendants.

5.Rule 612 - Refreshing Memory: If witness uses document to refresh memory, opponent can examine document, cross-examine about it, and introduce relevant portions.

Article VII - Expert Testimony (Rules 701-706)

1. Rule 701 - Lay Opinion: Admissible if rationally based on perception, helpful to jury, and not based on scientific/technical knowledge.

2. Rule 702 - Expert Testimony: Qualified expert, reliable methodology, applied reliably to facts, will help trier of fact.

3. Rule 703 - Basis of Expert Opinion: Can rely on inadmissible evidence if reasonably relied upon by experts in field.

Article VIII - Hearsay (Rules 801-807)

1. Rule 801(c) - Hearsay Definition: Out-of-court statement offered to prove truth of matter asserted.

2. Rule 801(d)(1) - Prior Statements: Inconsistent (if under oath), consistent (to rebut recent fabrication), identification statements.

3. Rule 801(d)(2) - Party Admissions: Party's own statement, adoptive admissions, authorized statements, employee statements, co-conspirator statements.

Rule 803 Key Exceptions:

(1) Present sense impression

(2) Excited utterance

(3) State of mind

(4) Medical treatment statements

(6) Business records

(8) Public records

Rule 804 - Unavailable Declarant: Former testimony, dying declarations, statements against interest.

COMMON OBJECTIONS GUIDE

Making Objections

Timing: Object before witness answers or immediately after answer.

Form: "Objection, [ground]" - be specific.

Standing: Must have good faith basis for objection.

Standard Objections

Relevance Objections:

- "Objection, irrelevant" (Rule 401)
- "Objection, unfairly prejudicial" (Rule 403)
- "Objection, character evidence" (Rule 404)

Foundation Objections:

- "Objection, lack of personal knowledge" (Rule 602)
- "Objection, lack of authentication" (Rule 901)
- "Objection, hearsay" (Rule 802)

Form Objections:

- "Objection, leading"
- "Objection, compound question"
- "Objection, argumentative"
- "Objection, asked and answered"

Expert Testimony Objections:

- "Objection, improper lay opinion" (Rule 701)
- "Objection, unreliable expert testimony" (Rule 702)
- "Objection, beyond scope of expertise"

Responding to Objections

As Proponent:

- Offer alternative theory of admissibility
- Provide missing foundation
- Limit purpose of evidence
- Rephrase question

As Judge:

- "Objection sustained/overruled"
- "Counsel, approach the bench"
- "Jury will disregard"
- "Strike that from the record"

Strategic Considerations

When to Object:

- Evidence actually harmful
- Good chance of success
- Preserving issue for appeal

When Not to Object:

- Drawing attention to harmful evidence

- Weak legal basis
- Evidence coming in anyway

PRACTICE PROBLEMS

Problem 1

In a personal injury case, plaintiff seeks to introduce evidence that after the accident, defendant installed a guardrail where plaintiff was injured. Admissible?

Answer: No. Rule 407 - subsequent remedial measures inadmissible to prove negligence. Could be admissible to prove ownership or control if disputed.

Problem 2

Defendant charged with bank robbery. Prosecution seeks to introduce evidence that defendant robbed a different bank two years earlier. Admissible?

Answer: Not under Rule 404(b) to prove propensity. Possibly admissible to show motive, intent, identity, or common plan if prosecution can articulate specific non-propensity purpose and satisfy Rule 403 balancing.

Problem 3

Witness testifies: "John told me he saw the defendant hit the victim." Hearsay?

Answer: Yes. John's statement to witness is out-of-court statement offered to prove defendant hit victim (truth of matter asserted). Need hearsay exception.

Problem 4

In contract dispute, party offers photocopy of signed agreement. Original is in party's office filing cabinet. Admissible?

Answer: No. Rule 1002 requires original when proving contents. Original is available, so Rule 1004 exceptions don't apply. Must produce original or give satisfactory explanation.

Problem 5

Criminal defendant wants to call character witness to testify that defendant is "peaceful and non-violent." Permissible?

Answer: Yes. Rule 404(a)(2)(A) - criminal defendant can offer evidence of pertinent character trait. Must be reputation or opinion testimony under Rule 405(a).

Problem 6

Witness says: "I can't remember what happened." Attorney shows witness a police report to refresh memory. Opponent's rights?

Answer: Rule 612 - opponent can examine the document, cross-examine witness about it, and introduce relevant portions if document used to refresh memory.

Problem 7

Expert witness wants to testify about accident reconstruction based on police report that would be inadmissible hearsay. Permissible basis?

Answer: Possibly. Rule 703 - expert can rely on inadmissible evidence if reasonably relied upon by experts in field. Court must determine if accident reconstruction experts reasonably rely on police reports.

Problem 8

Party offers certified copy of birth certificate from state vital records office. Authentication required?

Answer: No. Rule 902(4) - certified copies of public records are self-authenticating. No extrinsic evidence of authenticity needed.

Problem 9

Witness testifies: "The light was red." Objection: "Hearsay." Ruling?

Answer: Overruled. Not hearsay - witness testifying about personal observation, not repeating out-of-court statement. Rule 602 personal knowledge required.

Problem 10

In murder case, prosecution offers victim's statement: "If anything happens to me, John did it." Victim unavailable. Admissible?

Answer: Possibly under Rule 804(b)(2) dying declaration if made under belief of imminent death about cause/circumstances. More likely Rule 804(b)(3) statement against interest if exposed declarant to danger.

Problem 11

Business records custodian testifies company computer system automatically generates invoices. Foundation sufficient under Rule 803(6)?

Answer: Need more foundation. Must show: regular business activity, regular practice to make records, made at/near time, source had knowledge, records kept in ordinary course, witness qualifies as custodian/qualified person.

Problem 12

Attorney asks: "When you saw the defendant's car speeding through the intersection, what did you think?" Objection?

Answer: "Objection, leading and assumes facts not in evidence." Leading suggests answer; assumes car was speeding without foundation.

Problem 13

Defendant convicted of fraud 8 years ago, sentence completed 6 years ago. Admissible to impeach defendant who testifies?

Answer: Yes. Rule 609(a)(1) - felony less than 10 years from conviction or release admissible subject to Rule 403 balancing for criminal defendants. Fraud involves dishonesty.

Problem 14

Plaintiff offers hospital record containing notation: "Patient states he was hit by blue car." Admissible?

Answer: Multiple hearsay. Hospital record may qualify under Rule 803(6) business records. Patient's statement may qualify under Rule 803(4) medical treatment. Need foundation for both levels.

Problem 15

Party seeks to introduce summary chart of 500 financial transactions. Requirements?

Answer: Rule 1006 - must show documents voluminous, cannot be conveniently examined in court, summary accurate, underlying documents available to opponent for examination.

FINAL EXAM TIPS

Systematic Analysis

Step 1: Identify the evidence issue (relevance, hearsay, authentication, etc.)

Step 2: State the applicable rule

Step 3: Apply rule to facts

Step 4: Consider counterarguments and exceptions

Step 5: Reach conclusion with brief explanation

Time Management

Multiple Choice: 1.5-2 minutes per question maximum

Essays: Allocate time based on point values

Issue Spotting: Hit major issues, don't get lost in minor details

Common Mistakes

Relevance: Remember Rule 403 balancing even when evidence relevant

Hearsay: Check for non-hearsay uses before looking for exceptions

Character Evidence: Know when door is opened and by whom

Expert Testimony: Distinguish lay opinion from expert testimony requirements

Authentication: Don't confuse with hearsay - separate requirements

Key Reminders

- Evidence rules are rules of exclusion with exceptions
- Burden usually on proponent to establish admissibility
- Judge has discretion under Rule 403 even when evidence technically admissible
- Consider multiple theories of admissibility
- Procedural requirements matter (notice, foundation, etc.)

Final Tip: Practice systematic analysis until it becomes automatic. Evidence law rewards organized thinking and careful rule application.

REFERENCES

PRIMARY SOURCES

Federal Rules of Evidence

Federal Rules of Evidence (2025 ed.). Administrative Office of the United States Courts.

Advisory Committee Notes

Advisory Committee Notes to the Federal Rules of Evidence. Federal Judicial Center.

Key Supreme Court Cases

- Daubert v. Merrell Dow Pharmaceuticals, 509 U.S. 579 (1993).
- Crawford v. Washington, 541 U.S. 36 (2004).
- Davis v. Washington, 547 U.S. 813 (2006).
- Frye v. United States, 293 F. 1013 (D.C. Cir. 1923).
- Kumho Tire Co. v. Carmichael, 526 U.S. 137 (1999).
- Melendez-Diaz v. Massachusetts, 557 U.S. 305 (2009).
- Old Chief v. United States, 519 U.S. 172 (1997).
- United States v. Abel, 469 U.S. 45 (1984).
- United States v. Owens, 484 U.S. 554 (1988).

Important Circuit Court Decisions

- United States v. Inadi, 748 F.2d 812 (3d Cir. 1984).
- United States v. McCollum, 732 F.2d 1419 (9th Cir. 1984).
- United States v. Reynolds, 715 F.2d 99 (3d Cir. 1983).

SECONDARY SOURCES

Treatises

- Mueller, Christopher B. & Laird C. Kirkpatrick. Evidence (6th ed.). Wolters Kluwer Law & Business.
- Weinstein, Jack B. et al. Weinstein's Federal Evidence (2d ed.). Matthew Bender.
- Wright, Charles Alan & Kenneth W. Graham Jr. Federal Practice and Procedure: Evidence (2d ed.). West Academic Publishing.

Practice Guides

- Mauet, Thomas A. Trial Evidence (7th ed.). Wolters Kluwer.
- Park, Roger C. et al. Evidence Law: A Student's Guide to the Law of Evidence (4th ed.). West Academic Publishing.
- Rothstein, Paul F. et al. Evidence in a Nutshell (6th ed.). West Academic Publishing.

Law Review Articles

- Friedman, Richard D. "Confrontation: The Search for Basic Principles." 86 Georgetown Law Journal 1011 (1998).

- Imwinkelried, Edward J. "The Next Step After Daubert: Developing a Similarly Epistemological Approach to Ensuring the Reliability of Nonscientific Expert Testimony." 15 Cardozo Law Review 2271 (1994).
- Kaye, David H. "The Dynamics of Daubert: Methodology, Conclusions, and Fit in Statistical and Econometric Studies." 87 Virginia Law Review 1933 (2001).

OFFICIAL SOURCES

Federal Judicial Center

- Federal Judicial Center. Manual for Complex Litigation (4th ed.). Federal Judicial Center.
- Federal Judicial Center. Reference Manual on Scientific Evidence (3d ed.). Federal Judicial Center.

Department of Justice

U.S. Department of Justice. Criminal Resource Manual. U.S. Department of Justice.

Bar Examination Materials

- National Conference of Bar Examiners. Multistate Bar Examination Subject Matter Outlines. NCBE.
- Uniform Bar Examination. Evidence Outline and Study Guide. NCBE.

PROFESSIONAL RESOURCES

- American Bar Association Section of Litigation. The Litigation Skills Course. American Bar Association.

- Federal Practice Committee. Federal Rules of Evidence: A Fresh Review and Evaluation. American College of Trial Lawyers.

Note: All primary sources reflect current law as of 2025. Ensure to verify current authority and recent amendments when applying these materials in practice.

www.ingramcontent.com/pod-product-compliance
Lightning Source LLC
Chambersburg PA
CBHW071555210326
41597CB00019B/3251
* 9 7 8 1 0 8 8 0 3 0 6 6 0 *